T0381004

NUMBER'S GAME

DURIME ZHERKA

authorHOUSE®

AuthorHouse™
1663 Liberty Drive
Bloomington, IN 47403
www.authorhouse.com
Phone: 833-262-8899

Published by AuthorHouse   02/14/2023

ISBN: 979-8-8230-0116-8 (sc)
ISBN: 979-8-8230-0115-1 (e)

Print information available on the last page.

Any people depicted in stock imagery provided by Getty Images are models, and such images are being used for illustrative purposes only.
Certain stock imagery © Getty Images.

This book is printed on acid-free paper.

Because of the dynamic nature of the Internet, any web addresses or links contained in this book may have changed since publication and may no longer be valid. The views expressed in this work are solely those of the author and do not necessarily reflect the views of the publisher, and the publisher hereby disclaims any responsibility for them.

NUMBERS' GAME!

Slowly, slowly the grey cloud was moving its curtains and was opening space for bright rays of golden sun. Looked that cloud was forced to open that space while it knew that power of golden sun, while did not want to fight with heat so in silence was going away.

At that time one crew of white birds were flying with happiness while were chirping and the sun were doing bright their white color of their feather.

The trees looked were feeling the warm of Sun and their green leaves got bold in their color. Multicolor flowers opened their petals and all nature was in harmony with golden Sun.

Some blue glass buildings were playing with each other while were breaking and turning to each other the golden Sun's rays through their glass.

The different advertises in front of those blue glass building lost their importance, in this rainbow created by blue color glass and golden Sun rays that like flux in intercalary way were hitting the eyes of people.

On top of one glass building was one big monitor that was showing in different sequence times different numbers.

Those numbers were keeping their secret, their mystery, were counting people, states, cities, moneys, rivers, mountains, fields, different businesses, or corporations, but simple really were numbers with deep secret.

Some people careless were walking on wide sidewalk, some others were watching this big monitor with those numbers that were moving so fast in infinity. Some of them have simple curiosity some of them knew that moving of numbers maybe.

But monitor was moving fast and the different numbers were following each other behind. Like these numbers in monitors were moving fast on sidewalk so much people that were leaving their space to others behind while were creating one wave in moving like longer line.

All the street was dynamic the warm of Sun was giving so much positive energy, the moving of numbers in monitors looks like was in race with moving of people on sidewalk in front of blue glass building.

Moving of numbers on monitors and people on sidewalk surround with positive energy was sign of life that Universe was creating in this beautiful day in infinity.

Who can calculate how much rays ultraviolet the Sun is sending in second in our planet and giving so much life to people, plants, flora and fauna all around our environment, but this beautiful day is for sure that Sun loves people while is greeting them with its warm energy up and is making their life bright.

While I see this beautiful view, I thought what is the mystery of these numbers of monitors that are moving fast, what represents, what is showing up, what game is for our mind?!

I started to see very carefully this monitor, while numbers like in calculator, were creating one numbers' game when some numbers were disappearing and some others were coming with full speed, some were coming single, some were coming double, some came triple some in big number unimaginable.

Those strange numbers that from their size looks so small are giving so much power, to people, Corporation and states, their mystery I want to know. I started to see their rounding moving in sequence time, I thought this job will explode my mind.

I started to see their moving, and their probability how many times one numbers was coming in front of me. But the numbers understood my plan to discover their mystery they started to move in diffuse way, with numbers in crew, it was impossible for me to understand for the moment the number's game true.

Came number one that I do not like is single one, followed by number two that is weak unit, three and four came like solid, but five and six were moving with speed, seven came proud like famous number too, because of seven planets discovered until this moment true, after number eight that is claiming for magical wondering objects in our planet nine and ten were closing this unit.

In time came in line one hundred, one thousand with some power itself while one million and one trillion came with super power in this screen.

I started to think for all those units, I thought it is right for this big number to be proud because everything in our planet's live is based in numbers for everything and everywhere.

The amount of numbers is changing the health, are changing the economy, environment, population demography and all the world's life in infinity.

How much are influencing the big numbers in our daily life.

There are many phenomena, that when are happening in big number are changing people's life or town city or state demography.

Different conflicts in different countries of the world creating moving of people in big numbers to another place, this moving is creating vacant to first place and over population to place that are arriving. Immigration of these people creating foundation for so many changing in social life, about rules and laws of welcome country.

Every changing is coming in progressive way. People are learning new language, are integrating with new way of life and new concept of life too.

Big numbers of cold days are creating big movement of big crowd of birds from cold places to warm places.

Big numbers of insects are creating big damages of Agriculture's plants.

Big numbers of different countries that are accepting same program of system life is creating one strong union of those countries that is turned in system after.

Big numbers of super products to some countries is bringing big export to others countries too.

Big numbers of profit to some countries is bringing big expansion to others countries that some time is bringing big conflicts and movement of big numbers of people outside of their countries.

So, with those so many good things and so many different conflicts in different countries so many famous mathematicians can't put in order the big money of this game to establish situation, by inflations or expansion or movement of people around world.

But strangely this electronic monitor is continuing with super speed this game in numbers in infinity while is bringing so many different older and new phenomenon and is giving enthusiasm to people in very strange way.

Same situation are creating and the super huge numbers of stars in Universe that with their light in dark sky are giving some romantic feeling, dreaming and enthusiasm to people of Earth planet.

As estimated that are 2 trillion galaxy and some theory are claiming for 10 trillion galaxy while in our galaxy are more than 100 billion stars that this super huge number that we can name septillion or quadrillion are giving one big impact with their light because of their huge number and why they are so far away. Far away.

But how are affecting the stars in our life? We all are connected to the planet and the stars that are surrounding us.

We have one deepest and closest connection with planets that are in our solar system. Every one of those planet and stars are influencing direct or indirect to our life.

But how are influencing the planets and stars to our life. Our Universe is governed by four major forces as science is resulting that are:

".... Gravity, electromagnetism, nuclear - strong, and nuclear- weak."

Only two of them gravity and electromagnetism are two forces that make planets and stars to influence to us.

So, if the planets and stars are affecting to us is because of one or two of them. Those two forces gravity and electromagnetism are influencing things over distance.

There are some theories, about this energy, one named ether theory, that universal force inherent in that are forming what science named

"Empty space" that is metaphysic and alchemical theory, while another theory is about electric Universe theory.

This theory based in research science evidence based on plasma physic. This theory is the science of space as an electrically charged field in which all matter it is in turn charged and suspended and connected that.

In our system, stones, crystals, metals, color, Earth, air, water, fire Akash ourselves, our planet and all our Universe all contains Energy. It is this energy that permit, that allow everything in Universe to make its function.

This Energy is beyond religion beyond any theory or explanation. Is this energy that we feel affinity to the stars and so many times during evening we are doing our wishes for to full fill our desires.

This energy is making to activate our deepest desires while we are doing question and we are waiting answer by Universe when we are doing our wishes those evening.

People are attracted by stars on the sky

Every one of us have tried to wish during beautiful evening when the sky is full with stars for any very interesting and lovely desire, or intime, desire that we have while we do not see any open gate in real life.

So, this energy is influencing you, them and not exception me.

So, this energy is matter of stars and sun too.

it is stated and for that reason that energy cannot be created, nor destroyed, only transformed, we also made up of the same energy as our sun and the stars above.

1. But how are affecting the numbers in our body and our health too. If we can exposure or taking light to our face or our arm and our hand, about 10 – 15 minutes, two or three times a week it is enough for people to enjoy vitamin D boosting benefits by Sun.

    Sunlight is affecting so much to hour health and mental health too, so decreased of sun exposure is associated with drop in serotonin levels in level in our body that can lead to major depression with seasonal pattern.

    Sunlight and darkness trigger release hormone of brain to people. Exposure to sunlight is thought to increase the brain release of a hormone called serotonin.

    Without enough sun light or exposure, the serotonin level can go low and this is leading to major depression with seasonal pattern known as Seasonal Affective Disorder (SAD). This form of depression triggered by the changing of season.

2. The light that effects serotonin it is triggered by sunlight that goes through eye and specific in retina while this kind of depression we can experience in winter - time when the days are shorter.

3. So, decrease of serotonin is increasing melatonin that make us to sleep.

4. One main treatment for this kind of depression due to this connection with sun light and seasonal pattern is light therapy also known as phototherapy.

We can take light therapy box in home that the light from the box mimics natural sunlight while is stimulating the brain to make serotonin and to reduce excess of melatonin.

As we know the human's brain is operating its activity by neurons. According to many estimates the human brain contains around 100 billion neurons (give or take a few billions).

Also as is reported by neuroscience at the mother womb, brain cells grow at an outstanding rate of 250.000 neurons per minute.

Neurons are not identic, but differ in size, shape and others characteristic.

However, the main part of neurons is same.

Parts of neuron are three.

1- <u>Dendrite.</u>

Dendrite are thin branches of the beginning of each brain of cells. Those branches are creating surface while are taking information from neurons and are sending to the cell body. The total numbers of dendrite to each neuron differs.

2- <u>Cell body.</u>

Cell body also referred as soma (RNA) or acid ribonucleic, it is a polymer molecule essential in various biologic roles in coding, decoding, regulation and expression of genes. (RNA & DNA are nuclear acid).

Cellular organisms use messenger RNA (mRNA) to convey genetic information (using the nitrogenous bases

8

of Guanine, Uracil, Adenine, and Cytosine, denoted by letters G. U. A, C) that direct synthesis of specific proteins.

*** Many viruses encode their genetic information, using an RNA genome. ***

So science's people know encode of genetic like using RNA, genome of viruses but strangely, they can find fast to destroy viruses that are giving death to people as happened with covid 19 that gave death more than 4 million people around the world during 2019 - 2021.

The cell body is an important part of overall structure of neuron.

3- <u>Axon.</u>

An axon is an elongated fiber – like structure. It carries on information from cell – body and transmit to further. Usually all neurons in brain poses only long Axon.

The length of the Axon is directly proportional to how fast it transmits its information. At the same time, most axons are also covered by myelin sheath. It is a fatly substance which provides insulation for the transmission of information.

This sheath also helps the Axon to transmit information at a fast speed.

Neurons' function.

The basic function of neuron in the brain is to transmit information. This is the role performed by all types of brain cells. The following description simplifies this function.

1- Brain cells receive information in the form of signals. These signals enable us to see, smell, feel or taste.

2- The neurons process the incoming information. These cells determine whether the signals need to be passed or not.

3- The neurons pass on the received information to target cells. These may be other neurons, muscles, cells or glands. The target cells then perform the suitable reaction in response to the receive signal.

Types of Neurons.

Neurons in the brain are divided into three main classes.

These are discussed below:

Sensory Neurons.

These cells receive information from the sensory organs, system which then performs the suitable action.

A simple example of the function of sensory neurons is when we touch something hot our arms pull away from the hot object in an instant.

This is because the information passed on the sensory neurons which forward it to the target cells in the muscles.

Motor Neurons.

These cells receive information from other neurons. These signals are then passed on the target cell including the muscles, glandes or other organs.

Interneurons.

This type of brain cell is found only in central nervous system (CNS)

Are the most common type of neurons.

These are responsible for connecting different types of neurons with the brain or the spinal cord.

Interneurons receive signals from sensory neurons or other interneurons.

These signals are then transmitted to motor neurons or interneurons.

How neurons work.

Neurons in the brain transmit information with the help of electrical signals known as action – potential and chemical messenger – known as neurotransmitters.

A summary of the entire process is presented below:

1- A signal or information is received by the dendrites either from the sensory organs or other neurons in the human brain.

Dendrites with numerous branches can receive a large amount of information within "seconds".

2- The received information is transmitted within the brain cells and then on the next neuron or target cell.

This transmission is carried out by Axon. The signal passes along an Axon in the form of an action potential.

3- The connection between the end of Axon of one neuron and the receptors of the next neuron is called a "Synapse".

Information is passed between two neurons through this synapse with the help of neurons transmitters. These chemical messengers are released by the Axons.

4- Eventually the signal reaches the target cells in order to produce an appropriate response in the form of a muscle's contraction or the secretion of hormone.

Some facts very interesting amazing facts about neurons.

1- Totally numbers of neurons in the brain of human is around a hundred billion.

2- Inside mother's womb brain cell grow at an outstanding rate of 250.000.00 neurons per minute.

3- The longest axon in the human body extends from the tip of the toe up to the neck. It measures fifties feet in length.

4- Typically, the diameter of one neuron ranges between 4- 100 microns.

5- On average a signal bases through neuron at an amazing speed of 250 miles per hour.

6- If all neurons found in the human body are in line together, they would cover a total distance of a thousand kilometers.

To think those neurons in miniature are so decisive in life of human being, make us to believe about the "Super Perfection of Universe" creative job, about building body and brain of human. To study those neurons, calculate by their huge numbers needed huge numbers of months years or decades by scientists – people.

Universe has created those super miracles of neurons in brain of human, with super huge numbers, in very, very, small shape, with one perfection organize and operation, to give opportunities to science's persons in infinity to study and to work.

While we see these huge numbers of neurons in human brain with speed is coming to my mind how human's brain with those elements in miniature shape but with huge numbers can affect or can make decision life of human in our planet.

How this perfection systems of neurons can give some solution in future in our planet about so many important matters. How will be this intrigue game by those huge numbers in our daily life, this is one big mystery of our Great Universe. So many social life's matter in our planet needs solution for future. One of them is the density of population.

In demography the world's population is the total number of humans currently living and estimated to have reached 7.80.000.000.00 people or 7.8 billion people.

It took 2 (two) million years of human history for the world's population to reach 1(one) billion and only 200 (two hundred) years more to reach 7 (seven) billion people.

However, the world's population is still increasing and is projected to reach 10 (ten) billion people in 2050 and more 11 (eleven) billion in 2100.

Total amount of birth was highest in the late 1980, at about 139 (one -hundred- thirty-nine) million and as of 2011 were expected to increase to 80 million per year by 2040.

The median age of the world's population was estimated to be 30, 4 years, in 2018.

One big issue will come in extremely near future how will give the brain of human about this very important matter of feeding of the world's people. How human's brain with its neurons will create system to give normal food to 11 billion people in normal way.

How the human's brains with its perfection neurons- system will challenge this huge number of people, how the brain will put in light the full positive energy that is giving to it.

Anyway, I think all this perfection system of 100 billion of neurons with all their branches, in the human's brain, that are working without interruption have create some schemes to some scientist – people.

So, our brain will challenge this super huge number, or more specific this "Numbers – Game" about world's population to feed it.

Feeding the population for the world that is growing every day will not be easy task if is estimated to reach 11 billion people by 2100 so will be and more than 3.2 billion people than now.

But so many experts said that planet of earth will produce food enough to feed 11 billion people.

But there are coming two main problems about this matter, that are different with each other, while one is sustain of the food and other problem is that how much people or consumers will be able to afford this food.

So many science's people expert are thinking that humans cannot rely on one single food so must follow some different strategies. Those each strategy will move humans a little closer to toward closing the gap between the amount of food that they have and the amount of food that they need.

As experts are thinking are some strategies to help about feeding in future 11 billion people.

As a society tries to feed growing population it will pay close attention to the use Earth's resources or risk making situation worse.

- Beef is not sustainable food to eat. Because the greenhouse gas emission generated by the production of cheeseburger in the U.S.A. each year is about equal to the greenhouse gas emission from 6.5 million to 19.6 million SUVs over a year. So??!!

- This result came as research by Jamais Cascio in Institute of Future in Palo Alto in California.

- So, if we will think for the future to challenge the "Numbers-Game", about feeding growing population in future we need to change the way of eating, humans will be in need to eat differently than they are doing today, to use more vegetable which take much less energy to produce and less meat

- Another way is about eating meat that is not producing by an animal at all. Scientists have been working to develop cultural meat or synthetic meat in a lab.

- So many do not believe that lab grown meat would be truly and more sustainable than meat from cows.

- Cultured meat still required nutrients and so many researches explain that part of this meat will require the blood from fetuses of the cows.

  (According to a 2012 Discover Magazine post by Christina Agapakis a synthetist biologist at UCLA).

15

Some researchers have proposed that they could one day use alga to feed cultured meat. This is still experiment is not proved yet.

- Another way it is "Through less food away"!

One big inefficiency today's food system is how much food is wasted. One out of every four calories that is producing for human consumption it is not ultimately consumed because it is lost or wasted by people. This phenomenon we are seeing every day in our life so many times we are practicing this action.

People need to protect our Earth planet about everything and about reducing of wasting food all around. People need to protect the land where is cultivated different plants or industrial cultures because if we are using without limit the land, we will destroy one day.

As we know the land is good one in two years not to be planted,

(...so everywhere are numbers decisive...) this was my profession like high level agriculture specialist.

If we plant every year and we are wasting a lot food is not efficiency at all. We need to protect our Earth planet for current and future generation too. 56 % of global food lost in the world and wasting occur in developed world.

- Another way it is "Aquaponics". One idea of sustainable food's production is based on an ancient concept called Aquaponics.
- This concept is about creating system that combine producing of fish farming with plant farming in water.

- The fish fertilize the plant and the plants clean water for the fish. Really this theory is not new, and this experiment is not new because:

- Aquaponics is practiced like experiment late in 1980 in Albania in Mollas' s farm Elbasan, bordered with farm where I have worked in Gostima.

- It was great experiment in some HA with perfections about system of water's tubes for creating this basin of water, separated some Ha in corner of field from others part of field of crop also perfection of shape square.

- It was perfection service about fishes and plants in water. It was great at all. Veterinary person that got training outside of Albania for this research – experiment, was doing perfection job every day about notices or data. So, this is proven like theory in Albania.

- Really this idea of Aquaponics appears to have arisen hundreds of years ago, when farmers in Southeast Asia found that they could add tilapia to their rice paddy field to improve production yields.

- Another way is "Farming Vertical". Some have proposed taking farming into the sky. So, this theory is about growing up the crops in vertical farms. There are some positive and negative points about that:

- Positive points are:

- Food producing in vertical farm would not be in danger of being lost due to extreme weather that maybe is bringing worse and danger event.

- Food producing in vertical farms would not need to be shipped thousands of miles because the farm will be inside cities themselves.

- Negative point:

- Some researchers have argued that the cost of lighting in door vertical farms would be expensive.

- This theory is not proven yet widely, but really some aspects in miniature has started because so many has bought some textile bowls with small material of ground inside, to plant seeds of tomatoes hanging on wall of home or balcony and to produce and grown tomatoes by lighting by sun or electric lighting, me too, I tried.

- It is especially important to improve crops production worldwide, while effort should be made to improve crops' production specific in some are of our planet like in Africa and Asia.

So, this "Numbers – Game" by Universe still challenge until now the human's brain.

All the elements of Universe are getting sometimes shrink about their lights with so many problems of humans in Earth planet while they are sending so much positive energy and light to stranger humans' brain.

But all phenomenon that are derivates of Universe's energy cannot resolve problems of Earth planet's humans. So many raining is coming on ground but so many deserts are all around in our planet, so neurons have a lot to do in their "valuable home" – brain of humans.

Also, tons of raining water that Universe is sending through water condensation to our lovely Earth planet specific 100

18

cm on surface of earth never can escape the level of human's tears for not solution.

So many opportunities are coming by all minerals underground, but humans cannot find nutrition's – food.

So many forests are creating in centuries, about 30% of surface land of Earth planet so 40 million sq.km, are covered by forests, but it is difficult to find oxygen or produce oxygen also to use oxygen by people in needs.

71 % of surface of Earth planet is covered by water while ocean hold above 96, 59% of Earth's water but all around our planet so many humans are missing water to drink in their daily life.

Billion stars in Universe are watching us with big wondering while are sending with 299, 792 km/sec their speed of light, to us on Earth planet, for uncapable position to use positive energy that Universe is sending to us and to put in our service.

Stars are getting shocked about the superpower country on Earth planet the most beautiful by nature and relief the U.S.A. that has 5.680.000 sq. miles surfaces or 9.150.000 sq.km or more specific 1.9 billion acre, with density of population 94 people per sq. mile or 36 people per sq. mile (with population 325 million) or more specific.

Really the last estimate is showing that the U.S.A. has 2. 27 billion acres of land while federal government owns around 640 million, so 28% of totally territory while 92% acres of federal government's land are in 12 western states.

So, if we can calculate as experts say in normal way to live 5- 6 people per acre supposed that in the U. S.A' s land to live and more than 400 - 500 million people but,

.... Really, all are crying complaining, yelling and screaming about other people that are coming to live and enjoy this very beautiful country, that Universe has decorated with all wonderful mountains, hills, field rivers, and oceans while is decorating during spring and summertime with green covers by trees and green grass while colorful flowers with their blooming is designing around.

So, this "Numbers – Game" still capricious with humans non capable to perform their duty on Earth planet and society.

"Numbers – Game "is dancing around us with irony while is moving its numbers extremely fast, because we have lost our vision to see in detail its numbers what value has in our life.

Earth's humans are doing mixer the real value numbers with their remarkably interesting and strange feelings of profit while are not watching all possibilities for good life around.

Some people are justifying their action of accounting with different theories while are hiding their super selfish feeling about profit.

With some strange technical terms and sweet words are making legitime their accounting action while are hiding their illegal super selfish feeling in society.

Also, some quite simple action is putting in strange way to see create image that is difficult to achieve or performing it.

So many loudly noise is about Health insurance very strange, when people were living in empiric time, they did not have restriction for different group of community not to have right for health or healing but with the time everything changed but Universe is giving positive energy for all same it is not making divide.

20

So, about those strange health insurances, that is creating big issue for health of people are about 950.000 physicians plus so many others medical services person, and so many in hospitals, plus so many so many huge Hospitals in numbers about 7742 in U.S.A.

With those physicians is about one doctor for 342 people, but health care insurance is so much expensive that and the stars from the sky will get scared to know.

To enter in big game to challenge the "Numbers – Game" we can give to this one big simple calculation freely for super selfish:

People 325.000.000.00 x $5 for person infant until to very older age= $1.625.000.000.00.

From those people 74 million are children in the U.S.A. and 54 million are older people in the U.S.A. until 2020.

Totally, are 128 million people that are in need for service health care most of all the time.

325.000.000.00 – 128.000.000.00 = 197.000.000.00 adult people.

Let's; do one probability than 10% of those adult people needs health service so 19.700.000.

197.000.000.00 – 19.700.000.00 = 177.300.000 healthy adult people

177.300.000.00 x $5 = $886.500.000.00 per months.

$886.500.000.00 x 12 months = $ 1.063.800.000 these are reserve profit for insurance in future in the U.S.A.

And if will do $ 10 per person is reasonable and super huge profit to go for recovery for different medical equipment or medicine or whatever in hospitals.

With this calculation Earth's humans can challenge this stranger capricious" Numbers – Game".

So many theories are about our health care, really is conglomerate of so many sensors that five of them are so important like touch, sight, hearing, smell, taste. But what is showing to us this strange "Numbers – Game" about those numbers of sensors?

Touch.

- Touch is thought to be the first sense that humans develop to different object. If we are not touching any objects, we never know how soft, or strong those objects are or what shape they have.

- But how many objects we have create in our lovely world, by touching different stones, wood of trees, and oil underground, while we turned all those objects functional and worth in our daily life.

Sight.

- Sight, or perceiving things through the eyes, is a complex process.

- Sight or vision is the capability of the eyes to focus and detect images of visible light. There are 1530 colors as described by Natural Color of System.

- What about how many colors we can see or make difference with our eyes?!

- It is not establishing the numbers of colors in nature, but it is known or estimated that the human eye can differentiate, distinguished or recognize perhaps maybe about 10 million colors, while digital computer are known to generate up to 128 – bit color that's about 3 with 38 zeroes behind it.

- One favorable color in our planet is green color, this is the one of the most common colors in nature as most trees and vegetation are green due to chlorophyll a chemical of plant use to convert sunlight in energy, also there are known 295 green color.

- So, this green color is symbol of so many positive things, that are showing us for green space, also is used like main color to financial statement, in some countries like in my native country Albania is symbol of hope etc.

- Another problem in this "Numbers – Game "is about how we are precepting the numbers of colors with our eyes. Let us see the Rainbow as we know are seven colors in it, like Violet, Indigo, Blue Green, Yellow, Orange and Red, but there are many more colors which are not visible in a rainbow.

- We are seeing only seven colors in rainbow because these colors are spectral colors, and there are present in the visible spectrum.

Smells.

- Humans may be able to smell 1 trillion scents (fragrance or aroma) according to researchers. Smell is our ability to detect scent – chemical, odor molecules in air too.

Taste.

- Taste or gustation refers to the capability to detect the taste of substance such as food. Sense of taste is sensory system that is responsible for the perception of taste flavor.

- Humans have taste receptors on taste buds, while there are 2000 – 5000 taste buds that are located on the back and front of the tongue others are located on the roof and back of mouth and in throat.

- Each of these taste bud contains 50 to 100 taste receptors.

- Taste receptors in the mouth sense the five taste modalities: sweetness, sourness, saltiness, bitterness, and savories.

Hearing.

- Hearing, or audition, is the ability to perceive sound by detecting vibrations through the ear. Humans have a range of frequencies of hearing compared to other species – between 20 Hz and 20 000 Hz. Frequencies above that range are known as ultrasonic and those below are known as infrasonic.

We are doing the perception of the world by our five sense, but those five sense work independent but are very close with each other in their activity.

If we do not see around nature, we can't create image in our brain, if we do not hear we can't give attention or analyze to different phenomenon same situation and if we do not see or read.

If do not smell we can't do perception of aroma or different cooking, but if we do not touch, we never can create in our brain idea how strong or soft it is any object or merchandise too.

All those five senses helping us in our daily life about different action. These five senses are preparing us emotionally about every situation.

While this number's game is continuing its capricious game with moving different numbers how is possible that people are not moving with speed their science's research to help population and to create good environment to our lovely Earth planet.

If the speed of signal by neuron in brain of human is 250 miles per hour, how is possible that brain of people is making slow speed its job for different phenomenon.

If all viruses {*** Many viruses encode their genetic information, using an RNA genome. ***}

that are coming in our planet by different sources, like environment, like animals, and after by people but as we see by Number's Game their source and solution is to "RNA"'s genome {Acid Ribonucleic} how is possible that Genetic – science's persons are not finding solution about those different viruses while so many tragedy in super huge number are coming in population of Earth planet, so for that all the stars in Universe, that are sending so much positive energy are getting shock about humans' activity.

So, numbers are playing their games in our daily life in persistence way, and the most 50 (fifty) influences science's people around the world are not able to change this persistence and why they have done so many discoveries by their research.

Their highest-level, great prize for their science's job can't stop that pride - game of numbers in humans 'life. So those numbers when they are going in high level of amount are changing in drastic way the life of people.

So, we must give so much attention and importance to every number that s appear in our life about every phenomenon. When appears number one only one time is sporadic but if this number one is repeated so many times for this sign that we must to think.

This is about every process in our life, like in our communication with other people about positive or negative outcome, or about pain in our body, about in education field about our grade or about weather.

We must understand when is number one, only one time is sporadic but this is sign to prepare but when this number one is repeating itself and is going to 2, 3 4, and more is not mor sporadic but is prognose that is telling us something will happen for good or bad in different process of our daily life.

Related to that if we have one small cloud in our communication with other person and this situation is repeating itself this is telling us that something will come negative, also for pain in our body if is repeating so many times this is telling us that that something serious is coming about our health. About education when grade is coming more than one time positive or negative, we can estimate our good or bad result about grade of school.

Also, about changing weather, when we see so many days in line with hot sun will tell us to take measures for irrigation. This situation will bring the phenomenon of drought of the land. In recent drought the majority of farm and so many streams and rivers are going dry.

A small reduction in rain falls results in a significant reduction in surface runoff, that is creating high evaporation losses in farms. In some countries around the world, a drought can cause all - out war because people cannot grow crops and cannot make living and are struggling to get food sources to allow them to survive as a result the wars can break out.

There have been many wars started because of droughts of the land, also so many civil wars were breaking out because of the drought.

1. Since happened drought all around the world half of population eat just one meal a day. By World Food Program's report in some countries around the world lives on less than $2 a day and the total expectancy is 65 years.

   The UN estimates 12 million hectares of land are lost to drought and desertification each year, a potential loss of 20 million tons of grain.

   (One hectare is 10.000 squares meters).

   The United Nations. predicts land and soil degradation will reduce production of the next 25 years by 12 % (percent) like leading to e 30% rise in food prices.

As result of drought there is the huge impact in:

1- Agriculture health.
2- Environmental.
3- Social and economic consequences.

If are coming so many days with heavy raining is telling us about flood, so we need to prepare collector channel to go through the water.

About 70.8% of earth's surface is water covered while ocean hold about 96.5 % of all earth's water.

Water exists in the air as water vapor, in rivers, and lakes in icecaps and glaciers, in the ground as soil moisture and in aquifers and if to us. Water never is sitting still. Land is 29.2% on earth planet.

The world has lost a third of its arable land due to erosion or pollution in the past 40 years with potential disastrous consequences as global demand for food source.

Numbers like symbol are playing their mysterious game in front of us about every phenomenon of our life so we must give them one huge importance and attention.

According to information by Intergovernmental Panel on Climate Change (IPCC) the rate of soil erosion in many areas of the world is up to 100 times faster than the rate of soil information. It is also said the annual area of dryland in drought had been increasing at more than 1% (per cent) every year in the last 50 years.

Water and wind erosion are the world primary causes of land degradation that are responsible for about 84% of the global extend of degraded land that is making excessive erosion one of the most significant environmental problem of worldwide.

1- Rainfall and flood can create huge erosion of soil.

2- Wind erosion is a major geomorphological force, especially in arid and semi-arid regions.

Wind: It is also a major source of:

1- land degradation,

2- evaporation,

3- desertification,

4- harmful airborne dust,

5- and crop damage—especially after being increased far above natural rates by human activities such as:

6- deforestation,

7- urbanization, and agriculture.[21][22] {Wikipedia online erosion of soil}

Wind is creating deflation and abrasion,

Deflation is the lifting and removal of loose material from the surface by wind turbulence.[10][11] It takes place by three mechanisms:

1- traction/surface creep,

2- saltation,

3- and suspension.

- Traction or surface creep or soil creep is a process of downward progression of rock or soil down in low grade.

- Saltation that created by fluid wind or water and is process of removed material like sand to the field or desert in short distance.

- Suspended it is heterogeneous that makes mixture of fluid with sediments material.

Traction or surface creep accounts for 5- 25% of deflation so remove of material.

Suspension account 30- 40 % of deflation.

Saltation account for 50 – 70 % of deflation (13) {Wikipedia online erosion of soil}

Abrasion of soil is process that suspended material of soil and give big impact to solid object or material

Wind erosion is much more severe in arid areas and during times of drought. For example, in the Great Plains, in U.S.A. it is estimated that soil loss due to wind erosion can be as much as 6100 times greater in drought years than in wet years.[26]

Really erosion is natural process where rocks are broken down by natural forces such as wind or water. There two main of erosion chemical when rocks chemical composition is changing when iron or limestone are dissolved due to carbonation and physical erosion describes the process of rocks changing their physical properties without changing their basic chemical composition.

Removal of rocks or soil as clastic sediment is referred to as physical erosion this is different and contrasts with chemical erosion where soil or rocks material is removed from an area by dissolution.

So the numbers' game is giving us one big figure what they can do with their power, and about erosion. So many rain, so many flood, so many wind and so many activities by humans can create big erosion of the soil that to create itself got thousand years. But erosion is starting slowly, slowly, and if is not prevented with different measures is going fats and is sending down massive impact solid material.

For this in agriculture we have created system against erosion.

In farm in Gostima, Elbasan, in Albania where I worked like agriculture specialist we have created terrace all around the hills while we were studying every year how percent were losing soil during autumns, winter, and spring time and so we were calculated to make more deep percentage of terrace to all hills until to send in zero point erosion and we achieved that goal, on the hills that we were planting grain or tabaco.

While erosion is a natural process, human activities have increased by 10- 40 times the rate at which erosion is happening globally.

One of the main impacts of climate changing is polar melting. The rise in temperature empowers the greenhouse effect and the thawing of the ice mass especially at the North Pole, causing a rise in sea level which already has been noticed in so many coastal areas of earth planet and is giving so many consequences.

The melting of the north pole is directly related to the increase in greenhouse gas emission, particularly carbon oxide (CO2).

Since 1970 when satellite records began the relationship between the increase in CO2 concentration in parts per million(ppm) could be appreciated, that is showing the correlation as well as global temperature increase and the disappearing of ice surface.

In 1971 with concentration of 337 ppm and temperature rise of 0.41 grade Celsius, changed report of ice mass and CO and by preindustrial era.

In 2016 the ice mass surface took up 4.68 million km2 due to the temperature increase (+ 1.1. grade C), because of the preindustrial era and rise of CO2 concentration that in this time has reached 401ppm.

That means that since was starting record of melting with image has taken from space the North Pole has lost 35% of its ice.

Multiyear ice is thicker and has survived at least one melt season while first year ice is thinner. Also, artic sea usually reaches its minimum around mid, September each year.

In 2018 the national snow and ice data center noted that the amount of multi- year ice remaining this summer was sixth lowest record.

Global warming is the most serious problem that can affect our lives. All our activity, like using usage of fosil, fuels that we are doing every day cause the life of animals and humans endangered.

The most ice - cold places on earth are also affected by global warming, that are causing problems of life of animals and humans living around.

This bad effect of global warming to the two poles is giving direct effect to the world.

But how is playing their game the numbers about our environment of earth planet daily life in front of our eyes?

This game of numbers is showing to us about 6 (six) big impacts and effects of global warm in north and south pol.

1– The Ice Melting.

The phenomenon that is happening now which is direct by global Warming is the melting in North Pole.

It is considered to be one of the disastrous effects of global warming. Since in 1970 that satellite records concentration of Carbon Dioxide in part per million (ppm) that I was in 337ppm with temperature 0.41grade C increase North Pole lost about 7.2 million square kilometers of ice.

The conditions were not getting better also after 2016 the north Pole lost an additional 4.68 million km2 due to increase temperature.

2–   Many animals starting moving somewhere.

The change of climate is affecting the condition of environment that is making all animals living inside their zones leaving the areas. In this situation the animals that are living around the area of North and South Poles have no other choice than move to the colder areas.

Because of this changing climate the animals are forced to live and to maintain their population they would move to the others area in North or South Poles side, because of ice melting phenomenon that is happening.

3–   Floods will be everywhere.

One of the effects of rising sea - levels is flood. When ice in north and south Poles is melting there is rising in sea level.

This is bringing one bad phenomenon to maritime areas, floods.

The sea levels in average have been increased about 23 cm since 1980 and in every year, there is an increase on sea level about 0.13 inches.

The flooding disasters would lead to many people to evacuate and leaving their dear hometown for they do not know how long.

When flood is becoming regular disaster at that case inhabitant will leave their environment for a while like in Indonesia

4–   Rising Sea Level.

Global warming is bringing the effect of ocean salinity also from both ice melting in two poles North and South is bringing the rising of Ocean level.

This phenomenon not only causing floods which disrupt the people's activities but will increase on sea level can destroy the marine ecosystem as well this will bring result of leading erosion and diminishing the habitant of many animals.

To protect land from this rising level – sea in some countries like Jakarta, are creating seawalls and to some others are creating plantation like in Bali.

5– Reducing population of animals greatly.

The effect of global warming in ocean levels may bring destruction to many animals' habitants around the world. The rising of sea level may cause to destroy of shore ecosystem as well.

Many animals including the fishes and birds will lose their homes also reducing the people greatly.

As the result of this situation so many animals in colder areas like Adelie Penguins have suffered a lot from global warming. Because of decline in most of part of Antarctic Peninsula region made them to leave their areas. A lot of them already has lost because of this condition.

6– Causing more storms worldwide.

Another bad phenomenon of global warming between others that are happening anytime, is that this phenomenon may lead to more destructive storm and typhoons. They will destroy everything in their path.

Florence hurricane was a powerful and long-lived Cape Verde that caused catastrophic damage in the Carolinas in September 2018, primarily as a result of freshwater flooding due to torrential rain.

Florence hurricane it was a destructive hurricane that came as result of this climate changing condition.

This hurricane made that everyone to evacuate from risky areas like North and South part of Carolina. If the global warming keeps affecting the climate, more destructive hurricane would likely to occur.

Also, hurricanes Katrina that landfall at august 29, 2005 and Rita landfall at September 24, 2005 devastated south Louisiana claiming 1, 800 lives, destroying more than 200.000 homes and 18.000 businesses.

While in New Orleans in metropolitan area storm surge from Hurricane Katrina breached the city's level protection system at several points, 80 % of the city was left underwater and thousands were stranded on roof tops and in shelters- of the last- resort.

Hurricane Katrina damaged many buildings and lives. The storm was the most - deadliest and costliest ever to happen to America.

Damage was $ 126 billion, that cost $100 billion to rebuild, that really, they still building and this current time this day.

This hurricane was category 5 that hit Louisiana in august 29, 2005. It was the most destructive natural disaster in U.S. history. It impacted 93.000 square miles. Its' storm surge crested at 27 feet.

Hurricane Katrina was massive before to made landfall. Its storm with wind 120 miles per hour that damaged has created escaped the damaged that has created hurricane Andrew at Monday 24th, 1992 that totally was $ 26, 5 billion.

Hurricane Andrew, was a small and ferocious Cape Verde hurricane that brought unprecedented devastation along a path through the Northwestern Bahamas, southern Florida peninsula and south – central Louisiana (Report 1993 by national weather service).

Hurricane Andrew was the strongest and most devastating hurricane on record to it southern Florida. It struck south Miami – Dade, county (then known as Dade County) during the pre - dawn hours on Monday, August 24th, 1992

So those 6 effects of Global warming on North and South Poles and all those consequences of those hurricanes through the numbers are showing up in strong way how important are numbers in our daily life.

Those numbers for those events are telling us that the game of numbers is so strong with game that are doing and are giving us direction in our life about improving it or changing it or protecting it by so many disasters.

As result of those disastrous event by climate changing or by global warming so many people emigrating to another countries. As report showed by the World Bank at March 2018 migrated 130 million people, and July 31, 2019, that has put forward projection for internal climate migration amounting to 143 million people by 2050 in three regions of the world.

This phenomenon by worsening climate changing will create a looming human crisis and threating development process in three densely populated regions of the world as estimated the new world bank group.

But with action to be taken like including global efforts to cut greenhouse gas emissions and development planning at the country level this very worse, scenario of immigrating of 140 million people could be reduced in drastic way until to 80 or more than 100- 110 million people.

The report by "Groundswell – Preparing for Internal Climate Migrate, is the first the most comprehensive and very important study to focus in climate change - impacts, internal immigration pattern and development in three developing regions of the World like: Sub – Saharan Africa, South Asia, and Latin America.

In those three densely populated regions it finds that unless urgent climate and development action must talk globally and nationally, because those three regions like:

Sub – Saharan Africa, South Asia and Latin America all together will deal in near future with tens of millions of internal climate migrants by 2050.

These are people forced to move from increasingly non – viable areas, crop failure, sea level and storm surges.

These "climate migrants" of those three densely populated regions and of other spart of Earth planet would be additional to the millions of people already moving from their countries for economic, social, political or other reasons.

This is one point that is bold to this report by this Organization

Off course we are seeing every year international moving and domestic moving, for all those reasons for economic.

In 2018, the top country of origin for new immigrants coming in the U.S.A. was China, with 149,000 people, followed by India (129,000), Mexico (120,000), and Philippines (46,000).

By race and ethnicity, mor Asian immigrants than Hispanic immigrants have arrived in the U.S.A. in most years since 2009.

In 1960, 84% of immigrants living in the U.S.A. were born in Europe, Canada or other North American countries while only 6%

were from Mexico, 4 % from Asia, 3% from the rest of the Latin America and 3 % from other areas.

There were a record 44,8 million immigrants living in the U. S.A. in 2018, making up 13,7% of the nation's population.

This represents a more than fourfold increase since 1960, when 9.7 million immigrants lived in the U.S.A. accounting for only 5.4 % of the total population.

Still Mexico remains the top origin country for the U.S.A. immigrant populations, with 11, 2 million from Mexico in 2017.

This figure accounts for 25% of all United states migrants and is followed by the next largest origin group of China which make up 6%, India with 6% too, and Philippines with 5% respectively of share of immigrants.

None of those problems driving from Central America is inevitable. Hundreds of thousands – and often over million – Mexican once sought to reach the United States of America, every year.

But this trend started to fall after 2007, and the number of Mexicans in the United States has dropped from 11.7 million to 10.9 million in 2010.

The number of immigrants from Central America (legal and illegal) has grown 28-fold since 1970, from 118,000 to nearly 3.3 million in 2018 — six times faster than the overall immigrant population.

In 2018, 87 percent of Central American immigrants came from three countries — El Salvador, Guatemala, and Honduras.

El Salvador is the largest sending country from the region, with 1.4 million immigrants in the United States, a 112-fold increase since 1970. Guatemala is second with 815,000, followed by Honduras with 623,000.

Based on prior estimates by the Department of Homeland Security, slightly more than half of El Salvadorans are in the country illegally, as are about two-thirds of Guatemalans and Hondurans.[1]

A large share of Central Americans struggles in the United States, but it is not because they are unwilling to work. In fact, 76 percent of working-age immigrants from the region had a job in the first part of 2018, compared to 73 percent of the native-born.

In 1970, 49 percent of Central Americans had not completed high school, compared to 42 percent of natives — a seven percentage-point gap. In 2018, 47 percent of Central Americans had not completed high school, compared to 6 percent of natives — a 41 percentage-point gap. (by Stephen A Camarota, & Karen Zeigler:')

Central American Immigrant Population Increased Nearly 28-Fold since 1970 November 1, 2018.

Nearly 19,000 unaccompanied children entered U.S. custody along the southern border in March, an all-time monthly high that has forced the president of the U.S.A. Mr. Joseph Biden - administration to house migrant teenagers in convention centers, camps for oil workers and a military base, according to preliminary government data provided to CBS News.

The historic number eclipses previous record-high migration flows of Central American teenagers and children that strained the government's border processing capacity under Presidents Barack Obama and Donald Trump in 2014 and 2019, respectively.

The previous all-time monthly high came in May 2019, when nearly 12,000 unaccompanied children arrived at the U.S.-Mexico border.

U.S. agents along the southern border carried out approximately 170,000 total apprehensions in March — a 70% increase from the previous month.

During time of former president Mr. Donald J Trump administration.

Through August of the current fiscal year, 2020 the Border Patrol apprehended (arrest or taking in custody) 457,871 migrants arriving as "family units." That was a 406% increase compared to the 90,554 family unit apprehensions during the same period the previous year 2019.

Migrant families from Guatemala, Honduras and El Salvador made up almost 92% of the total. Honduras and Guatemala both had more than 180,000 family members reach the U.S. this fiscal year 2020.

The number of unaccompanied minors arriving at the border also spiked this year.

Through August, the Border Patrol apprehended 72,873 migrant children. That's up 60% from the previous year and has already surpassed the record 68,631 apprehended in fiscal year 2014.

(BY CAMILO MONTOYA-GALVEZ, ADAM VERDUGO.) Nearly 19,000 unaccompanied children entered U.S. border custody in March — an all-time high.

But what about education of those immigrants that are coming in the territory of the U.S.A. in 1970, only 4% of Central Americans had at least a bachelor's degree, compared to 55 of natives – a one percentage point gap.

In 2018 to 10% of Central Americans had at least a bachelor's degree compares to 38 % of natives – a 28% percentage – point gap.So, the numbers are playing are continuing their game with speed in our earth planet with speed in every aspect of our life and economic too.

So, all this big moving of people in every corner of earth planet the numbers are showing their supremacy that March 28, 2020, according to the Air Action Group, the World's airline carried total of over 3 billion passengers in a single year.

While international Air Transport association has the figure at 2, 8 billion people that were traveling.

While in August 26, 2020, 39.8% of people travel internationally (Canada, Mexico and / or Caribbean (by Travel Leaders Group). 39.5% of people travel within their home state (Travel Leaders Group)

The numbers are showing with their game that in November 10, 2020 that 54% of people were traveling at least some of the time, compare with year 2017 that were traveling only 34%.

From those people solo travels are frequent travels. Also 46% of those are traveling three or more times per year. Travel for adventure beats out urban travel that 305 like adventure travel while only 23% favor urban travel.

39.5% of people travel within their home state (Travel Leaders Group). So, the Airline Corporation are playing giant role in business of every country int this planet.

As numbers are showing with their very beautiful and speed their game that billions of people that are traveling are bringing profit multiply of billions but those never are helping to reduce poverty in so many countries!

This is one big issue, that numbers with their game are not showing their secret that this super huge amount of money by billion travels, cannot reduce the poverty and so many epidemy or pandemic or different disease in system in every country or like global??!!

All those phenomena are related with education because those people that are moving from their home country to others country has one important reason for more better life and education of course plus so many others different reasons, politic, saving their life etc.

But as the numbers with their game moving so fast and showing that 1000 top Universities around the world that are covering 80 locations, compare with 5500 Universities around the world are preparing intellectual people to service to society.

Education levels vary between countries around the world. In general people in undeveloped countries do not have access to qualify education or education at all.

Those in developed countries have higher literacy rates and at least a basic high school education. According to the Global Partnership of Education, education is considered to be human right and plays crucial role in human, social and economic development.

Education promotes gender quality, promotes peace, and increases a person's chances of having more life opportunities

To think that from this pandemic affected 1,3 billion students, this is one figure that so many billion intellectuals are around the world but so many problems about medical, food, different crisis in different countries are not finding solution and this is another big issue that is coming by this very strange mysterious game of the numbers.

NUMBERS OF STUDENT AROUND THE WORLD.

In 2020, Australia had the greatest amount of international students compared to their entire higher education population with 31.3 percent of students being international.

Canada followed with a share of 23.7 students being international, while the United Kingdom ranked third.

India has the most Universities worldwide. According to data from July 2020, there were an estimated 4,381 Universities in India.

The United States had the second most Universities counting 3,254, followed by China with 2,595 Universities.

Harvard University was the top-ranked University in the world in 2021 with a score of 100 according to the Shanghai.

Ranking Consultancy group. Out of the top 50 ranked Universities, the United States had 28 different Universities on the list.

Several indicators are used to rank the Universities.

Number of alumni and academic staff winning Nobel Prizes and Fields Medals, highly cited researchers, papers published in Nature and Science, papers indexed in major indices and the per capita academic performance of the institution.

The highest scoring institution is assigned a score of 100 and other institutions are calculated as a percentage of the top score.

For the academic year of 2021/2022, the University of Oxford was ranked as the best university in the world, with an overall score of 95.7 according the Times Higher Education.

The California Institute of Technology, Harvard University, Stanford University, and the Massachusetts Institute of Technology rounded out the top five universities in the world for that year.

1- HARWARD UNIVERSITY U.S.A.100
2- STANFORD UNIVERSITY U.S.A 75.9
3- -UNIVERSITY OF CAMBRIDGE 70.6
4- MASSACHUSETTS INSTITUTE OF TECHNOLOGY (MIT) 69.5
5- UNIVERSITY OF CALIFORNIA BERKELEY. 66
6- PRINCETON UNVIRESITY 59.7
7- UNIVERSITY OF OXFORD'59.2
8- COLUMBIA UNIVERSITY 58
9- CALIFORNIA INSITUTE OF TECHNOLOGY.57.9
10- UNIVERSITY OF CHICAGO 54.7
11- YALE UNIVERSITY 53.7
12- CORNELL UNIVERSITY 50.3
13- PARIS CAKLAY UNIVERSITY.49.4
14- UNIVERSITY OF CALIFORNIA LOS ANGELES.48.9
15- UNIVERSITY OF PENSYLVANIA. 47.8
16- JOHNS HOPKINS UNIVERSITY. 47.6
17- UNIVERSITY COLLEGE LONDON.47.3
18- UNIVERSITY CALIFORNIA OF SAN DIEGO. 46.3
19- UNIVERSIRY OF WASHINGTON. 46.2
20- UNIVERSITY OF CALIFORNIA SAN FRANCISCO.44.6
21- ETH.ZURICH .44.4
22- UNIVERSITY TORONTO. 41.3
23- WASHINGTON UNIVERSITY IN ST. LOUIS.40.7
24- UNIVERSITY OF TOKIO. 40.7

25- IMPERIAL COLLEGE LONDON. 40.5

26- UNIVERSITY OF MICHIGAN ANN ARBOR. 40.1

27- NEW YORK UNIVERSITY. 39.6

28- TSINHUA UNIVERSITY. 39.5

29- UNIVERSITY OF CAROLINA AT CHAPEL HILL.38.1

30- UNIVERSITY OF COPENHAGEN. 37.7

31- UNIVERSITY OF WISCONSIN MADISON. 37.6

32- 31-DUKE UNIVERSITY. 36.5

33- 32-UNIVERSITY OF MELBOURNE. 37.1

34- NORTHWESTERN UNIVERSITY 36.5

35- SORBORNE UNIVERSITY. 35.7

36- THE UNIVERSITY OF MANCHESTER .35.7

37- KYOTO UNIVERSITY.35.6

38- PSL.UNIVERSITY.35.2

39- THE UNIVERSITY OF EDINBURGH.35.2

40- UNIVERSITY OF MINNESOTA
    TWIN CITY 35.1

41- THE UNIVERSITY OF TEXAS, AUSTIN. 34.8

42- KAROLINSKA INSTITUTE. 34.6

43- ROCKFELLER UNIVERSITY. 34.6

44- UNIVERSITY OF BRITISH COLUMBIA. 34.6

45- PEKING UNIVERSITY. 34.5

46- UNIVERSITY OF COLORADO AT BOULDER.33.8

47- KING'S COLLEGE LONDON.33.5

48- THE UNIVERSITY OF TEXAS SOUTHWESTERN,

49- MEDICAL CENTER OF DALLAS.33.2

50- UNIVERSITY OF MUNICH .33.2

51- UNTRECHT UNIVERSITY.33.1

It shows that our world will be inhabited by more and more educated people: while in 1970 there were only around 700 million people in the world with secondary or post-secondary education, by 2100 this figure is predicted to be 10 times larger.

Education is widely accepted to be a fundamental resource, both for individuals and societies. Indeed, in most countries basic education is nowadays perceived not only as a right, but also as a duty – governments are typically expected to ensure access to basic education, while citizens are often required by law to attain education up to a certain basic level.

Those numbers are providing an overview of long run changes in education outcomes and outputs across the world, focusing both on quantity and quality measures of education attainment; and then provide an analysis of available evidence on the determinants and consequences of education.

From a historical perspective, the world went through a great expansion in education over the past two centuries. This can be seen across all quantity measures.

Global literacy rates have been climbing over the course of the last two centuries, mainly though increasing rates of enrollment in primary education.

Secondary and tertiary education have also seen drastic growth, with global average years of schooling being much higher now than a hundred years ago.

Despite all these worldwide improvements, some countries have been lagging behind, mainly in sub-Saharan Africa, where there are still countries that have literacy rates below 50% among the youth.

11 FACTS ABOUT EDUCATION AROUND THE WORLD

1- As of 2012, 31 million primary-school pupils worldwide dropped out of school. An additional 32 million repeated a grade.[1]

2- In the sub-Saharan, 11.07 million children leave school before completing their primary education. In South and West Asia, that number reaches 13.54 million.[2] {education worldwide online}

3- While girls are less likely to begin school, boys are more likely to repeat grades or drop out altogether.

4- According to UNESCO, 61 million primary school-age children were not enrolled in school in 2010. From these children, 47% were never expected to enter school, 26% attended school but left, and the remaining 27% are expected to attend school in the future.

5- Children living in a rural environment are twice as likely to be out of school than urban children. Additionally, children from the wealthiest 20% of the population are 4 times more likely to be in school than the poorest 20%.

In developing, low-income countries, every additional year of education can increase a person's future income by an average of 10%.

Women who are less educated are having more children, on average 2.5 children, over the course of their lifetime when compared to more educated women, on average 1.7 children.

Women with a primary school education are 13% more likely to know that condoms can reduce their risk of contracting HIV/AIDS. An education can help decrease the spreading of this virus by promoting safer sexual practices.

53% of the world's out-of-school children are girls and 2/3 of the illiterate people in the world are women.

Education empowers women to make healthy decisions about their lives. For example, women in Mali with a secondary level education or higher have an average of 3 children, while those with no education have an average of 7.

The youth literacy rates in South America and Europe are among the highest with 90-100% literacy. The African continent, however, has areas with less than 50% literacy among children ages 18 and under.

According to that data in 2014 the estimate for all enrolled students in primary and secondary schools in the world was 1,287,078,204 (1.29 billion).

Primary: 719,059,053, Secondary: 568,019,151

BTW (By the way), These numbers seem to correlate nicely with the US Census 2014 estimate of the number of school age children worldwide

UNESCO, data 2010 shows ~750 million student.

In most developing countries teacher 30:1 is too small, even in private Indian schools closer to 50:1.

In 2017, there were over 5.3 million international students, up from 2 million in 2000 (UNESCO, 2019). More than half of these were enrolled in educational programs in six countries:

The United States of America, the United Kingdom, Australia, France, Germany and the Russian Federation.

Internationally, more students than ever are attending college.

Between 2000 and 2014, the number of students in higher education globally more than doubled to 207 million, according to a paper (pdf) published by UNESCO, together with the International Institute for Educational Planning and the Global Education Monitoring Report.

The Ranking of World Universities (ARWU) 2021World University rankings by Times Higher Education 2021/202 World University rankings by reputation score, by Times Higher Education 202 Forbes ranking of the best U.S. colleges 2021, by debt and median 10-year salary

The highest scoring institution is assigned a score of 100 and other institutions are calculated as a percentage of the top score.

The numbers' game is continuing with speed its trick but between other is showing up one very great information by statistic about medical field that will leave speechless everybody.

The Universe gave opportunity to earth planet that everybody to enjoy the treasures of its and to have full treatment about health. But numbers's game is showing something different that we want to see for real.

There are 10 to 15 million doctors in the world. The World Health Organizations estimates there is a shortage of 4.3 million physicians, nurses and other health workers in the world.

This shortage can be attributed to the fact that there are limited medical schools in the developing world. In addition, these few medical schools have a small capacity for admission of students, and upon graduation, qualified medical personnel in developing countries often migrate abroad in search of better remuneration and improved working conditions.

However, developed countries, such as the United States, United Kingdom, Canada, Australia and Germany, are also facing a shortage of doctors.

Doctors make a difference. Studies have found the more primary care doctors to have in every area, the longer people will live. The trouble is that is a shortage of healthcare workers in the world.

According to the World Health Organization, some countries have less than one physician for every 1000 people living within their borders. It is estimated that there is a global shortage of about 4.3 million healthcare professionals around the world today, and that number is increasing.

Despite the impressive numbers of the leaders, there are only 1.13 doctors for every 1,000 people in the world today. For some countries, the rates are even much lower still.

This shocking revelation has led the World Health Organization to estimate that in the next decade or so, there will be a global shortage of about 4.3 million healthcare workers when including physicians, nurses, and medical technologists.

This World Health Organization is claiming for more numbers of doctors and is in need for 6 million nurses specific for current pandemic

"Covid – 19" through period time 2020 – 2021.

Really problem is not only to medical staff that needed but, is the time of preparing prophylactic measures before.

So, this preparing time before needed support by different nonprofit organization and so much by media to give education to people in every country all around the world.

One very important and great job has done media that is giving all those information to people that can change for better their life.

2021 Social media Usage. As January 2021 there were more than 3. 96 billion social media users in the world.

Considering that are 7 billion people globally more than half of the global population is currently using social media in one form or another??!!

Social media is not just changing the way we communicate – it's changing the way we do business, the way we are governed, and the way we live in society.

There are six observations and predictions for the way social media is changing the world from experts from the "Global Agenda Council"

1. **Across industries, social media is going from a "nice to have" to an essential component of any business strategy.**

Social media skill is no longer considered the responsibility of a small team in the newsroom but social media affects the way the whole organization runs. Because of digital marketing or new customer service communication channels media already is spreading to the businesses beyond the newsroom. In digital time is not only newsroom about spreading media but people all around the world are participating in easy way.

2. Social media platforms may be the banks of the future.

In future is transforming banking relationship in very significant way, from improving customer service to allowing users to send money to others via online platforms. New financial technology companies are using social media to help people simply to open new account. Social media can impact people's ability to get loan too.

Can happen in future that people to pay rent or to make investment through their favorite social network. Also, media has created possibility to make signature by online for different contract and in publishing books too before one decade. I am using this process of signature by online for my books in the last one decade before with great publishing AuthorHouse.com.

Also has started already before one decade since 2009 that different people to sing by online from Europe to U.S.A. or all around the word about different transaction about buying property. I had this occasion with my relative from Europe that did sign of buying property in Fort Lauderdale by electronic. So they did electronic signature from over there (Brussel – Belgium).

So, the foresee by Mr Richard Eldrige Chief Executive Officer of Lenddo Pte Ltd. became reality about social media of transforming the banking relationship.

But this process this operation will not be without problems, because the biggest challenge will be maintaining of security standards about ensuring customers knowingly provide personal information. Banks also must be agree or to implement with sophisticated social media policies.

3. Social media is shaking up healthcare and public health,

Social media has played one big role about public health through virtual doctor's visits on Skype. Also, social media helped different people that were suffering from the same illness to stay in touch with each other.

Social media helped so many groups of people to share their information in open public health. But this situation has and another negative side, because during one disease outbreak, because non expert of media maybe share information rapidly has health agencies.

So, health agencies must have plan to be prepared in time to be able to respond to any misinformation and counter or to support accurate information shared via -social.

These two ways of health agency has positive side of sharing so fast information but maybe has another negative side about sharing misinformation by social media.

4. Social media is changing how we govern and are governed.

Digital media has changed the way of governing, because so many citizens can be source of new ideas, plans and initiatives in an easier way than before.

Before the politicians and government officials had to travel to interact with citizens, now online provide possibility and platform for direct input on government initiatives.

So, in the future through social media expected more and more leaders to embrace this type of very transparence governance, and will be easier to interact and communicate with others every politician also congressmen and senators etc.

5. Social media is helping us better respond to disaster weather.

So many people are using digital media to contribute about any natural disaster weather that is going to happen wherever they are.

Digital responders are using their technical skills, their time as well their personal network to help with their sharing information for humanitarian aid during natural disaster or human created catastrophe. Those digital responders will help close the gap in worldwide disaster response

6. Social media is helping us tackle some of the world's biggest challenges, from human rights violations to climate change.

Syria war, The Arab spring, Miramar tragic events about protest of people, are, caravan of immigrants from Central America through Mexico to come to the U.S.A., immigrant people from Afghanistan and middle east that are going in border between Belorussia, and Poland to use like transit to go to Germany and so many others event are the best - known examples of how the media can change the world.

Always the numbers are playing their magical strange game while are telling their power about different new phenomenon that are e happening around the world.

The big numbers are speaking by itself. The huge numbers of immigrants from central America made that two countries Mexico and U.S.A. to see more seriously and to make some big changing about immigration rules and to adopt with new situation.

About those events last this decade more important is about more than just bringing together activists; it is also about holding human rights violators to account. Satisfaction is about sharing by media about those events, like war of bad treatment in protest or bad treatment about immigrants is because social media has increasing potential to be used as evidence of war time and human right violation.

"Following verification and cooperation with forensic reconstruction by prosecutors those videos are potential evidence that may one day brought before an international court."

"Following verification and forensic reconstruction by prosecutors and human rights advocates, these videos are potential evidence that may one day be brought before an international court."

Another matter that it is so important in our Earth planet is about climate change, that social media is providing sources with their video to people to see about decision maker by Government and different Corporations that are affecting for bad our environment and all of us.

So, social media is providing for people for public space to participate in influencing, or disallowing or blaming decision about damaging environment.

This is creating a way for people to connect local environmental challenges and to find solution too, to large scale, and in wide way that will affect all of us like as a Global community.

So many big numbers of damaged of environment demand so big numbers of activist to participate and environmentalists to change situation for good, so always numbers are playing their very interesting game about this matter too.

The world is interconnected. Everyday math shows these connections and possibilities. The earlier young learners can put these skills to practice, the more likely we will remain an innovation society and economy.

So, interconnection in different points of our earth planet between different countries and communities is creating so many new possibilities about improving our life depended to tradition and to innovation. Math through its numbers is speaking strongly by itself about influencing in life of Earth planet, and about life of people.

But what is telling to us this numbers' game about our environment of our lovely Earth planet?

Plants are an inspiration, and they are at the center of our lives. For marriage we celebrate with a bouquet, and at a funeral we remember with a wreath. From the banana in our lunchbox, to the homes we construct, the fuels we burn and the air we breathe, plants are an integral part in our living world.

We may have put humans on to the moon, yet we still don't have a definitive list of all plant species on Earth. In 2002, governments that were parties to on the "Convention on Biological Diversity "adopted the "Global Strategy for Plant Conversation".

But to compare the giant job that has done Charles Robert Darwin about evolution of species until he published his book in 1859 about "On Origin of Species".

But in this modern time that we are leaving these science people of biology they are so much behind if we are calculating the modern technology about research or about operation. So needed so much to do by them and by all.

During the Darwin's time did not have this modern technology and all this huge information worldwide, but he did in his initiative with his expenses with his super passion for biology and science while was traveling with his expenses for more than five years around the Earth planet.

While today in modern time with modern technology are so many supplies and equipment to make easy research or travel or experiment but people are thinking and doing only routine job for one good wage or let's say high payment but maybe is missing in their heart and chest the huge and good passion about it, about this specific science.

But who was Charles Robert Darwin (February 12, 1809 – April 19, 1882)? He was an English naturalist, geologist, and biologist, he is best known for his contribution on for his contribution to evolutionary biology. {(6) Charles Robert Darwin Wikipedia online}

In his theory he gave proposition that all species of life descended from common ancestors and whit theory now is widely accepted and considered like fundamental concept of science. So, during his interpretation to other science persons of biology in his time in London, U.K. he introduced his scientific theory about "Evolution" it si result of process of "Natural Selection"

During natural selection all species are struggling for their existence in different environment. His theory is so much practical in modern time and is similar with artificial selection, but anyway his theory is used in current time about selection of livestock or about different plants to adopt more with new environment.

Charles Robert Darwin for his theory has been honored by burial in Westminster Abbey, also he is the most influential figures in human history.

So definitely his studying about theory of evolution Charles Robert Darwin published like evidence in his book in 1859 with title "On Origin of Species"{(11) (12) Charles Robert Darwin, Wikipedia online}.

During 1870s the scientific community and majority of educated public at last they accepted the theory of evolution as fact, but some opponent in science biology gave to him only a minor role to nature selection.

Only in period time of 1930 to 1950 when emerged the modern evolutionary synthesis that all science people accepted that natural selection was the basic mechanism of evolution. {(13) (14) Charles Robert Darwin Wikipedia online}.

<u>Definitely the theory of evolution that is scientific discovery of Charles Robert Darwin, it is the unifying theory of life's sciences, that is explaining the diversity of life.</u> {(15) (16) Charles Robert Darwin Wikipedia).

After that was created like logo term theory of Darwinism.

But what happened with Darwin during his life:

1- His passion and interest for nature made that he to neglect his medical education at the university of Edinburgh (while annoyed his father for that).

2- Darwin helped to investigate marine invertebrates.

3- During his studies in university of Cambridge (Christ's College) that he went to study for Bachelor of Art degree, that encouraged his passion for natural science.

4- Charles Robert Darwin after leaving Sedwick in Wales he spent five days with student at Barmouth after he return to his home on August 29, friends.

5- Charles Robert Darwin had to stay at Cambridge until June 1831, while he studied "Paley's natural theology of evidence of the existence and attributes of Deity that was published in 1802.

This book made one argument for divine design in nature, that was explaining adaption as God acting through the Law of nature.

{(39) Charles Robert Darwin Wikipedia, online}

6- Charles Robert Darwin read John Herschel's new book, "Preliminary Discourse on the Study of Natural Philosophy (1831).

This book described the highest aim (focus) of natural philosophy that understanding that such a law through inductive reasoning based on observation,

7- Charles Robert Darvin also read Aleksander von Humboldt's Personal Narrative of scientific travels in 1799 – 1804, that inspired with a

"a burning zeal" (great energy or enthusiasm in pursuit of a cause or an objective) to contribute, Darwin planned to visit Tenerife with some classmates after graduation to study natural history in tropics

In preparation, he joined Adam Sedgwick's geology course, then on 4 August travelled with him to spend a fortnight mapping strata in Wales.{[40][41] Charles Robert Darwin Wikipedia, online}

8- After leaving Sedgwick in Wales, Darwin spent a few days with student friends at Barmouth, then returned home on 29 August while he received one letter from Henslow proposed him as a suitable (if unfinished) naturalist for a self – funded supernumerary place on HMS Beagle with captain Robert FitzRoy while was emphasizing that this [position was really for gentleman rather than for "e mere collector"

(being nothing more better than what is specified)

The ship was to leave in four weeks on an expedition to chart the coast line of South America. {(42) (43) Charles Robert Darwin, Wikipedia online)

So, his father Robert Darwin (May 30, 1766 – November 13, 1848) was an English medical doctor, who today is best known as the father of the naturalist Charles Darwin decided one plan for his son Charles Robert Darwin.

He was a member of the influential Darwin–Wedgwood family.

He objected to his son's planned two-year voyage, regarding it as a waste of time.

While Josiah Wedgwood II, the brother – in - law of Robert Darwin convinced his mind (to Robert Darwin) to agree and to fund his son's participation in this activity. {[44] Charles Robert Darwin, Wikipedia online}

Darwin took care to remain (to go on) in a private capacity to retain control over his collection, intending it for a major scientific institution. {[45]

Charles Robert Darwin Wikipedia online}

HMS Beagle was a Cherokee-class 10-gun brig-sloop of the Royal Navy, one of more than 100 ships of this class.

The vessel, constructed at a cost of £7,803 (roughly equivalent to £638,000 in 2018), was launched on 11 May 1820 from the Woolwich Dockyard on the River Thames.

So, again Numbers' Game again are showing their power about this ship that people at that time and British Kingdom spent so much of building this ship for expedition for explorer and for science in future.

This HMS Beagle ship took part in celebration of the coronation of king George iv of the United Kingdom, passing through the old London Bridge and was the first rigged man of war (the first armed ship) afloat upriver of the bridge {(2)(3), Charles Robert Darwin, Wikipedia online}

HMS Beagle after made changing about interior structure and took part in three survey expedition.

The second voyage of HMS Beagle is notable for carrying the recently graduated naturalist Charles Darwin around the world.

While the survey work was carried out, Darwin travelled and researched geology, natural history and ethnology onshore. He gained fame by publishing his diary journal, best known as The Voyage of the Beagle, and his findings played a pivotal role in the formation of his scientific theories on evolution and natural selection. {[4][5] Charles Robert Darwin Wikipedia online}

1- During his five years voyage on HMS Beagle Charles Robert Darwin established himself like geologist that observation and theories supported the concept of geological change.

2- Publishing his journal of the voyage made Darwin so famous and popular author. {(18) Charles Robert Darwin Wikipedia, onlone}

3- Charles Robert Darwin puzzled by the Geographical distribution of wildlife and fossils he collected on the voyage.

4- Charles Robert Darvin began detailed investigation while in 1938 conceived his theory of natural selection.{(19) Charles Robert Darwin Wikipedia, online}.

5- He discussed his ideas with several naturalists, he needed time for extensive research, and his geological work had priority. {[20] Charles Robert Darwin, Wikipedia online}

6- He was writing up his theory in 1858 when Alfred Russel Wallace sent him an essay that described the same idea, prompting immediate joint publication of both their theories. {[21] Charles Robert Darwin Wikipedia online}

7- Darwin's work established evolutionary descent with modification as the dominant scientific explanation of diversification in nature in 1871{[13] Charles Robert Darwin, Wikipedia, online}

8- He examined human evolution and sexual selection in The Descent of Man, and Selection in Relation to Sex, followed by The Expression of the Emotions in Man and Animals (1872).

9- His research on plants was published in a series of books, and in his final book, The Formation of Vegetable Mould, through the Actions of Worms (1881), he examined earthworms and their effect on soil.{[22][23] Charles Robert Darwin, Wikipedia, online}

During one studied or examination about research of species, among the 16 adopted targets for 2010 was, first, a working list of all known plant species.

Botanic gardens in the UK and US are leading in this research and the plant list currently stands at an estimated 380,000 species – and it's still not complete.

It is very important to know the theory of Darwin about evolution and selection of species because it is of struggling and surviving of different species in different environment.

This theory also is in correlation and with human's life about their struggling adopting and surviving for so many reasons in different new unknown Environment.

Darvin's theory it is so useful in agriculture's science about selection of different seeds or plants in new environment.

With activity of Charles Robert Darwin people must to understand that in that time was not modern technology that is speeding process of research or travel or organized of information in computer, but life was more empiric but the beating heart of science people and their feeling about exploring something new and good for life of human was so strong and in high level.

At that time people about exploring were sacrificing their time their own money, their life in wild unknown environment, but they achieved their goal, because they had mission and they performed their mission.

So the Numbers; Game is showing strongly the power of numbers in human's life, about amount of money, about amount of days months and years in their daily activity.

As Andrea Wood has said one beautiful phrase that:

"Plants are key of life in earth planet ".

1-Plants supply food to nearly all terrestrial organisms, including humans. We eat either plants or other organisms that eat plants. Plants maintain the atmosphere.

They produce oxygen and absorb carbon dioxide during photosynthesis. Oxygen is essential for cellular respiration for all aerobic organisms.

Plants recycle matter in biogeochemical cycles. For example, through transpiration, plants move enormous amounts of water from the soil to the atmosphere.

Plants provide many products for human use, such as firewood, timber, fibers, medicines, dyes, pesticides, oils, and rubber. Plants create habitats for many organisms.

A single tree may provide food and shelter to many species of insects, worms, small mammals, birds, and reptiles.

Plants are creating one very beautiful and full diversity of our environment.

Also, plants are creating diversities of fragrance with petals of flowers about different perfumes that everyone like, also plants are creating one very good environment about like digging in minimized of the ground by microorganisms that are creating and feeding themselves with their roots and their lymph liquid, of their wood body or whatever or with their chlorophylls of their leaves.

Plants where are drying are creating one very testing and wonderful food for livestock that pressed in silos and used for winter, time.

Plants are creating one strong diversity, about wild plant and cultural plants, there are creating one symbiose or the unity between good and bad in our Universe, that is phenomenon that is happening in our society of humans being too.

At least and wild plants before centuries are source of continuing life of humans in our earth planet.

The first-ever report of its kind presents mounting and worrying evidence that the biodiversity that underpins our food systems is disappearing – putting the future of our food, livelihoods, health and environment under severe threat.

The report points to decreasing plant diversity in farmers' fields, rising numbers of livestock breeds at risk of extinction and increases in the proportion of overfished fish stocks.

Biodiversity for food and agriculture is all the plants and animals - wild and domesticated - that provide food, feed, fuel and fiber. It is also the myriad of organisms that support food production through ecosystem services – called "associated biodiversity".

This includes all the plants, animals and micro-organisms (such as insects, bats, birds, mangroves, corals, seagrasses, earthworms, soil-dwelling fungi and bacteria) that keep soils fertile, pollinate plants, purify water and air, keep fish and trees healthy, and fight crop and livestock pests and diseases.

Of some 6,000 plant species cultivated for food, fewer than 200 contribute substantially to global food output, and only nine account for 66 percent of total crop production.

The world's livestock production is based on about 40 animal species, with only a handful providing most of the meat, milk and eggs. Of the 7,745 local (occurring in one country) breeds of livestock reported globally, 26 percent are at risk of extinction. Nearly a third of fish stocks are overfished, more than half have reached their sustainable limit.

Information from the 91 reporting countries reveals that wild food species and many species that contribute to ecosystem services that are vital to food and agriculture, including pollinators, soil organisms and natural enemies of pests, are rapidly disappearing.

For example, countries report that 24 percent of nearly 4,000 wild food species – mainly plants, fish and mammals - are decreasing in abundance. But the proportion of wild foods in decline is likely to be even greater as the state of more than half of the reported wild food species is unknown.

The largest number of wild food species in decline appear in countries in Latin America and the Caribbean, followed by Asia-Pacific and Africa. This could be, however, a result of wild food species being more studied and/or reported on in these countries than in others.

Many associated biodiversity species are also under severe threat. These include birds, bats and insects that help control pests and diseases, soil biodiversity, and wild pollinators – such as bees, butterflies, bats and birds.

Forests, rangelands, mangroves, seagrass meadows, coral reefs and wetlands in general – key ecosystems that deliver numerous services essential to food and agriculture and are home to countless species – are also rapidly declining.

Leading causes of biodiversity loss.

The driver of biodiversity for food and agriculture loss cited by most reporting countries is: changes in land and water use and management, followed by pollution, overexploitation and overharvesting, climate change, and population growth and urbanization.

In the case of associated biodiversity, while all regions report habitat alteration and loss as major threats, other key drivers vary across regions.

These are overexploitation, hunting and poaching in Africa; deforestation, changes in land use and intensified agriculture in Europe and Central Asia; overexploitation, pests, diseases and invasive species in Latin America and the Caribbean; overexploitation in the Near East and North Africa, and deforestation in Asia. **Biodiversity-friendly practices are on the rise**

The report highlights a growing interest in biodiversity-friendly practices and approaches. Eighty percent of the 91 countries indicate using one or more biodiversity-friendly practices and approaches such as: organic agriculture, integrated pest management, conservation agriculture, sustainable soil management, agroecology, sustainable forest management, agroforestry, diversification practices in aquaculture, ecosystem approach to fisheries and ecosystem restoration.

Conservation efforts, both on-site (protected areas, on farm management) and off-site (gene banks, zoos, culture collections, botanic gardens) are also increasing globally, although levels of coverage and protection are often inadequate.

"**Biodiversity Friend**" is a VOLUNTARY standard open to all agricultural farms with plant production (family farms, cooperatives, large-scale distribution) that believe in a sustainable agriculture model, with low environmental impact and integrated into the landscape.

Biodiversity-friendly cities should have many different tree species supporting multiple ecosystem functions. Urban tree species themselves are an important component of floristic diversity. This diversity friendly is practiced in so many countries of this world to help and improve environment, where people are working about planting trees, land and agricultural plants too.

Most of all this diversity friendly is developed in urban area about trees and floristic.

In Albania during period time 1970 -1980, people started to create on huge space while planted orange, lemons and olive by

Government's program, and created the pearl of South Albania, created riviera of Albania.

So, with this friendly diversity they covered all the hills aside the Jon - sea and in interior land the most beautiful place in planet that was continuing until to beautiful beach city of Saranda and to Ksamil.

This project was one the most giant project of Albania's Government at that time that created this green necklace from Vlora to Saranda and Ksamil, where the blue sky was sending by its lovely hot sun the hot rays to those hills and aroma of those beautiful plants, like orange lemons, citrus and olive tree, were kissing the very blue Jon while were making the white waves to come in lazy way close to the sound or to the rock like drunk by those wonderful smells.

The specter of color like deep blue of Jon - sea with green space of those trees with red roofs of the different houses and up the blue sky was the most wonderful image that anyone can create or see.

Looked that Universe has painted through the hand of human the most beautiful painting on earth planet and this wonderful painting named "Albania's Riviera" that no one can find to another country of this Earth planet.

I have worked after graduated High School in July, 1975 with other students in Ksamil, Sarande, during summer time (July month), two months before to go to University so was program of former Government of Albania to work voluntary about this green space so we practiced this friendly biodiversity.

It was organized by former Government that all youth people that finished high school to work in green space about planting trees from Vlora to Saranda and Ksamil inside relieve with hills and through the south coastline, during summer time, also in different village were students of different University of Albania.

Really it was one very giant and very beautiful job that gave so much good result in years to come plus created the most beautiful Environment.

This tradition of working voluntary by youth people and students of University, was continuing to others fields of agriculture or to build railway through country.

So, every year during four years University we had one month voluntary work in different field in Albania.

Biodiversity is the biologic variety and variability on Earth. Biodiversity is a measure of variation at the genetic, species and ecosystem level. This biodiversity it is different in different places of earth planet.

Biodiversity is richer near the Equator. The terrestrial biodiversity is greater near equator that is result of warm weather and has high primary productivity.

Biodiversity is richer in tropic. These tropical forest ecosystems cover only ten percent of earth surface and contain about ninety percent of the world's species.

In those forest that has so much productivity is result of the weather that every day is raining maybe one hour and is coming hot sun that is giving life to trees.

In the U.S.A. Marine biodiversity is usually higher along the coasts in the Western Pacific, where sea surface temperature is highest, and in the mi- latitudinal band in all oceans. There are latitudinal gradients in species diversity.

Diversity tends to cluster in hotspot and is increasing through the time but will be likely to slow in the future as a primary result of deforestation.

It encompasses the evolutionary, ecological, and cultural processes that sustain life.

Rapid environment changes typically cause mass extinctions. More than 99.9 percent of all species that ever lived on earth, amounting to over five billion species are estimated to be extinct.

Estimates on the number of Earth's current species range from 10 million to 14 million of which about 1, 2 million have been documented and over 86 percent have not yet been described.

The total amount of related DNA base pairs on earth is estimated at 5.0 x 1037 and weighs 50 billion tons. It comparison, the total mass of the biosphere has been estimated to be as much as four trillion tons of carbon.

In July 2016, scientists reported identifying a set 355 genes from the Last Universal Common Ancestor (LUCA) of all organism living on Earth planet.

The most interesting is the fact of the age of the Earth planet that is about 4, 54 billion years. The earliest undisputed evidence of life on earth dates at least from 3. 5 billion years during the Eoarchean Era after a geological crust started to solidify following the earlier molten Headen Eon.

There are microbial fossils found in 3. 48 billion – year – old sandstone, in Western Australia. Other early physical evidence of biogenic substance in graphite in 3.7billion - year - old meta-sedimentary rock discovered in western Greenland.

More recently, in 2015 "remain biotic life" were found in 1. 4 billion - year – old rocks in western Australia. According to one of the researchers,

"If life arose relatively quickly on Earth… than it could be common in the Universe.

Since life began on earth, five major mass extinctions and several minor events have led to large and sudden drops in biodiversity.

The Phanerozoic eon (the last 540 million years) marked a rapid growth in biodiversity via the Cambrian explosion – a period during which the majority of multicellular phyl first appear.

The next 400 million years included repeated massive biodiversity losses classified as mass extinction events.

In the Carboniferous, rainforest collapse led to a great loss of plant and animal life.

The Permian - Triassic extinction event, occurred 65 million years ago and has often attracted more attention than others because it resulted in the extinction of the non – avian dinosaurs.

So, this Number's game is showing us the powers of its numbers about the past of our earth planet, about evolution of earth and about declined, deteriorated, or atrophied it.

But what is telling this Numbers' game during evolution of our earth planet depended by weather or different phenomenon of diversity of weather what brought the result?!

During this evolution under different circumstance of changing weather also by people's activity on earth planet happened one very important phenomenon that named "Deforestation".

DEFORESTATING

Half of the world's forests have disappeared. Privatization, trade liberalization and increased exports of meat and crops, such as soy and palm oil, have led to a massive increase in large-scale plantations, triggering further deforestation. Yet forests provide livelihoods for many local communities and indigenous peoples. They help to regulate our climate and are home to some of the most species-diverse habitats on earth. While the climate crisis has dominated the airwaves for a while now, the biodiversity crisis is at least as serious. These are multiple, interconnected crises, stemming from age old systemic failings. In 2019, scientific body IPBES brought to the fore the urgent need for "transformative change" to prevent biodiversity collapse, which would be disastrous for people and planet. As one example, the global coronavirus pandemic has tragically highlighted the risks of ecosystem loss for global public health.

In a bid to find an answer to this crisis, the United Nations Convention on Biological Diversity (CBD) is discussing a Global Biodiversity Framework (GBF) - effectively how to 'save' nature. The CBD is often referred to as the biodiversity equivalent of the climate talks, with the GBF nicknamed the "Paris Agreement for Biodiversity".

The CBD has a long history with indigenous peoples, who have a specific status within the convention. There is a working group dedicated to indigenous issues and there has been a lot of work on the knowledge of indigenous peoples and their relationship with biodiversity. Yet, this rich and invaluable history is getting lost in the current framework.

Boreal Forests.

Boreal forests consist mainly of coniferous trees. Coniferous trees, like pine trees and spruce trees, have seed-bearing cones (pinecones). Boreal forests are found almost exclusively in Arctic regions in Canada, Alaska, Finland, Sweden, Norway, and Russia.

Temperate Forests.

Temperate forests are forests that exist between the warmer tropics and the colder polar regions.

They change with the seasons. There are several types of temperate forests. So many should be familiar with temperate forests because these are the forests in Pennsylvania!

Tropical Forests.

Tropical forests have once major thing in common – they are hot! When you think of tropical places, you probably think about rainforests, which are very wet, but tropical forest can be dry too.

Think about which type of tropical forest has more trees. Below is a map showing where you can find tropical rainforests. Now that we have learned a little bit about 3 different forest types, let's estimate the number of trees on Earth. 2. Make a hypothesis! How many trees do you think are on the planet Earth right now? How did you come up with this number? The table example below shows the area that each forest covers on the planet Earth and the density of trees for each forest type.

TYPE OF FOREST.

FOREST TYPE,	AREA THAT IS COVERED BY EACH FOREST IN KM2,	AREA IN THE TERM OF THE U.S..A., TREE DENSITEY,	TREES / KM
TROPICAL	45, 465. 000	4,5 TIMES THE SIZE OF THE U.S.	28, 506
TEMPERATE	30, 648,000	3 TIMES THE SIZES OF THE U.S	23, 326
BOREAL	15, 390,000	1,5 TIMES THE SIZES OF THE U.S.	48, 690

1. Which type of forest has the highest tree density? To figure out how many trees there are on Earth for each forest type, multiply the area covered by the forest (column B) by the tree density (column D).

2. Tropical Forests, Temperate Forests, Boreal Forests

3. 45,465,000 km2x __ 28,506 trees/km2, = trees, TEMPERATE, 30,648,000x __ 23,326 trees/km2 TREEES/KM2, BOREAL FOREST, --------------

4. Now, fill in the table above with you answers, and add them all up to find the total number of trees in forests on Earth. 6. The number of trees in the world is approximately 3,040,000,000,000. Why might the number of trees on Earth in forests be LOWER than this number? Think about other places that you find trees that are not in forests... EXTRA!!! 7.

The number of trees on Earth has decreased by 46% since humans began cutting them down. Therefore, the 3,040,000,000,000 trees estimated to be on Earth represent only 54% of the number of trees it originally had. How many trees did our planet have before we started cutting them down? (Hint #1: this number should be BIGGER than 3,040,000,000,000. (Hint #2: Solve for 'x'.) 3,040,000,000,000 X 54/100

Every year from 2011 – 2015 about 20 million hectares of forest was cut down. Then things started to speed up. Since 2016 an average of 28 million. Since 2016 an average 28 million hectares have been cut down every year. That's one football field of forest lost every single second around the clock. 1 billion hectares cut down in 40 years. In just 40 years a forest area of the size of Europe has gone. Half of the world's rainforest has been destroyed in just one century. If we don't act and the current rates of deforestation continue, the world's rainforest will be gone in 100 years.

Deforestation major factor in global warming The clearing of forests is a big contributor to global climate change. About 20 percent of the world's greenhouse gas emissions come from the clearing of tropical forests. Since 2000, the loss of tree cover has added 98.7Gt to global CO_2-emissions.

In 2017, deforestation added about 7.5 billion tons of carbon dioxide to the atmosphere - almost 50 percent more than the all energy-related CO_2-emissions from the entire US.

Deforestation messes up the water cycle Trees are essential to the water cycle. In the rainforest ecosystem, over half the water is held within plants as absorbed rainfall and three quarters of the world's freshwater is supplied by forest catchments. So, when trees are cut down, the water cycle is destroyed as well.

Deforestation causes soil erosion

Without the roots of trees to anchor the soil, it washes away including the nutrients contained in the soil.

... and desertification

If soil erosion is not stopped it can ultimately turn the land into desert. The United Nations has labelled desertification as potentially the world's most threatening ecosystem change.

"The main reason tropical forests are disappearing is not a mystery – vast areas continue to be cleared for soy, beef, palm oil, timber, and other globally traded commodities."

Something really needs to change. The world population is growing by the minute and so is the global consumer class.

WORLD POPULATION 7.953 965 825

1. The total forest area is 4.06 billion hectares, or approximately 5 000m 2 (or 50 x 100m) per person, but forests are not equally distributed around the globe.

   More than half of the world's forests are found in only five countries (the Russian Federation, Brazil, Canada, the United States of America and China) and two-thirds (66 percent) of forests are found in ten countries.

2. There are numerous beautiful forests in the world, and collectively they cover about one-third of Earth's total acreage.

3. These forests provide the oxygen we need to breathe as well as sequester carbon, that confounding climate change catalyst. Forests also protect our world's water supply: When they disappear, we inevitably get **deserts**.

4. These incredible forests produce all sorts of food for us to eat, and provide medicines that have healed humans for centuries.

5. Despite these commonalities, the biggest forests in the world are impressively diverse. Each offers its own unique combinations of trees and understory plants. Each is home to a diverse array of animals, fungi, mosses, insects, and people.

6. While forests of every size are important to the health of our planet, sometimes we can't help but wonder how big they can actually get.

7. The more expansive forests can cover a surprising amount of square mileage, standing strong as some of the last slices of true wilderness left in our modern world. Let's take a look at the 10 largest forests in the world and examine what makes each of them unique.

10– Sinaharaja forest reserve.

Size: 34 square miles
Forest Type: Tropical Lowland Rainforest
Location: Sri Lanka
Prominent Wildlife: Sri Lanka Crested Drongo and Green Pit Viper

9--- Indo - Nabillo Cloud forest

Size: 74 square miles
Forest Type: Cloud Forest
Location: South America
Prominent Wildlife: Quetzals and Basilisks

8-Kinabalu National Park8-

Size: 291 square miles
Forest Type: Mountain Rainforest
Location: Asia
Prominent Wildlife: Proboscis Monkeys and Rhinoceros Beetles

7-Daintree Forest.

Size: 463 square miles
Forest Type: Wet Tropics Rainforest
Location: Australia
Prominent Wildlife: Saltwater Crocodiles and Southern Cassowaries

6- Rainforest of Xhishuangbanna.

Size: 927 square miles
Forest Type: Tropical Rainforest
Location: Asia
Prominent Wildlife: Asian Elephants, Indo-Chinese Tigers, and Green Peacocks

5-Sundarbans.

Size: 927 square miles
Forest Type: Tropical Rainforest
Location: Asia
Prominent Wildlife: Asian Elephants, Indo-Chinese Tigers, and Green Peacocks

4-Tongass.

The Tongass National Forest (/ ˈ t ɒ ŋ g ə s /) in Southeast Alaska is the largest U.S. National Forest at 16.7 million acres (26,100 sq mi; 6,800,000 ha; 68,000 km 2).Most of its area is temperate rain forest and is remote enough to be home to many species of endangered and rare flora and fauna.

Tongass National Forest. Alaska's Tongass National Forest comprises a significant portion of the world's last remaining temperate rainforest. This spectacular 17 million acre region supports abundant wildlife, including such priority bird species as the Marbled Murrelet. Audubon's goal is to conserve intact, ecologically significant...

3-Valdivian Temperate Rainforest.

Size: 95,800 square miles
Forest Type: Temperate Rainforest
Location: South America
Prominent Wildlife: Southern Pudú, Kodkod, and Wild Boars

2-Congo Rainforest.

Size: 781,249 square miles
Forest Type: Tropical Rainforest
Location: Africa
Prominent Wildlife: Leopards, Okapi, and Hippos

Amazon rainforest.

Size: 2,300,000 square miles
Forest Type: Broadleaf Rainforest
Location: South America
Prominent Wildlife: Jaguars and Tapirs

ENVIRONMENT'S CHANGING HAS MOVED SO MUCH PEOPLE FROM THEIR PLACE AND TO IMMIGRATE TO ANOTHER PLACE OR COUNTRY TOO.

Environment's changing has moved so much people from another place or country to another place or country too.

So many social phenomenon that changed the world and created so many different events tragedy and big changing in people life in this planet.

Consequences of the First World War I

Death and destruction during the course of the war, 8 million soldiers died in total and 9 million civilians. In addition, the bombings destroyed 300,000 houses, 6.000 factories, 1000 miles of train lines and 112 coal mines.

World War I caused more damage than any other war before it.

9 million soldiers and as many civilians died in the war. Germany and Russia suffered most, both countries lost almost two million men in battle. Large sections of land, especially in France and Belgium, were completely destroyed. Fighting laid buildings, bridges and railroad lines in ruins.

World War I or the First World War, often abbreviated as WWI or WW1, was a global war originating in Europe that lasted from July 28, 1914 to November 11, 1918. Also known as the Great War or "the war to end all wars", it led to the mobilization of more than 70 million military personnel, including 60 million Europeans, making it one of the largest wars in history.

Also known as the Great War or "The War To End All Wars", it led to the mobilization of more than 70 million military personnel, including 60 million Europeans, making it one of the largest wars in history.

December 09, 2014 · World War One was one of the deadliest conflicts in the history of the human race, in which over 16 million people died.

The total number of both civilian and military casualties is estimated at around 37 million people. The war killed almost 7 million civilians and 10 million military personnel. Military and Civilian Deaths on Both Sides.

World War I generated major social changes, birth rates abruptly fell by the death of millions of young men. In addition to this, many citizens lost their homes and had to flee to other countries.

The role of women also changed, as they had to replace men in offices and industries. In this line, the rights of women, such as the right to vote, began to increase.

High social classes ceased to play such a dominant role in society as the middle and lower classes began to claim their rights after the war.

Effects.

#1 ETHNIC CLEANSING AND GENOCIDE

The *Armenians* had inhabited the *Caucasus region* of Eurasia for *close to 3 millennia* having taken up the *Christian faith* in the 4th Century AD.

Over the years the region shifted hands among its neighboring empires, and in the 15th Century was occupied by the *Ottomans*; making them *a small religious minority* in an Empire *ruled by the Muslims.*

As the Ottoman Empire crumbled in the decades leading up to WW1, *suspicion against the Armenians grew* and *brutal action was taken against those who protested against the empire.* Things came to a boil after the *Ottoman defeat*

History of Armenian is that they had inhabited the Caucasus region of Eurasia for close 3 millennia while they had Christian faith since 4th century ad. In 15 century was occupied by Ottomans that were turning them in small religious minority in that empire ruled by Muslim.

During WWI While the empire was taking power in decades, they have suspicion about Armenian that they did brutal action who protested again empire. When Ottomans defeat against

Russians in the battle of Sarikamish early of WWI The general of empire Enver Pasha publicly blamed his defeat on Armenian, that he supposed that they were cooperating with the enemy. {by "learnodo - new tonic. com" effects of WWI.

Armenian soldiers and other non- Muslims in the army very soon demobilized and killed by Ottoman troops while regular forces began mass killing in the villages. On April 24, 1915, close to 250 Armenian politicians and intellectuals were arrested.

By the end of the Great War the Ottoman Empire was ethnically cleansed of 90 percent of its Armenian population. Similar pretexts were also used against the Assyrians and the Greeks.

As of 2018, Turkey still denies genocide as an accurate term for the crimes while 29 countries have officially recognized the mass killings as genocide.

#2 REVOLUTIONS OF 1917–1923

The period of the time that was ending the "World War I" brought so many big changing like in Russia saw in February Revolution 1917, that fought monarchy and made Tsar to abdicate.

At that time the provisor Government that was formed was thrown by Bolshevik Revolution of October 1917, beginning the reign of communists in Russia.

So many countries around the world that inspired by the success of the Russian Revolution, uprising their activity in that political uncertainty time.

At 1918 as the war ended a socialist revolution happened to Germany that created environment to create left- leaning Weimar Republic that brought in power the Adolf Hitler's Nazi Party that seized power in 1930.

The other new movement was Irish war for Independence in 1919 – 1920, also another new movement on social life was Hungarian revolution in 1918 – 1920, the other was the Egyptian Revolution in 1919, also in Italy was movement Biennio Rosso also started so many movements of colonial revolts in middle east and in Southeast Asia.

Those movements or Revolution were most of them socialist anti colonial but there were most of them with short – lived, so did not have effect for long – term impact.

#3 LOST GENERATION

World War I was a catastrophic event in terms of lives lost in the history of the world. During fighting died 8 million around to10 million one among eight combatants. Also 5 million civilians were killed, with 15 million seriously wounded and 7 million permanently disabled.

Germany lost 15,1% of its active population, while Austro – Hungary lost 17.1% and France lost 10.5%. So, during this war no one can say that any country that was involves in this war, did not lose lives. During this war approximately 65 million combatants from 28 countries fought in conflict. So many people that were going in this world war I faced so much disillusionment among those that never returned.

So many of them went to the war believing of heroism and nobility but really, they faced only horrors of this war.

Until that time Europe did not see the war for 100 years while those who fought became known as "The Lost Generation" because they never fully recovered from suffering.

So, the "Number's Game" is showing during this war, its power to give one strong lesson to people of earth planet that war never is solution to resolve any social or economic in people life.

This is great experience and for the war now about Russia against peaceful Ukraine 2022.. Let's calculate with numbers the time is going more than 78 years, started this strangely war we can't say it was unpredictable, because the signs were showing itself by Russia because a lot of economic problems inside it.

But we can say that was unpredictable the mind or decisions of all politicians of Russia or more exact of all leaders of Russia in different levels.

Because to start one unreasonable war is not deciding one person but is deciding by union of leaders of this country. So, it was unpredictable this decision or action by leaders of Russia and never can accepted any justify by them and in century to come, plus, they are fighting with their people strange unbelievable.

So, the numbers are so much decisive in our life on Earth planet and "Number's Game" is showing tis capricious and pride for its power about every event in earth planet

#4 COLLAPSE OF FOUR GREAT EMPIRES

The economic, social, military and political pressures of WWI proved to be the *final death blow* for *four great monarchies* and *their empires*.

They were namely the *Hohenzollern,* the *Habsburg,* the *Romanov* and the *Ottoman.* These had dominated the political scene in Europe for centuries.

Russian – Japanese war, was fought between the Empire of Japan and the Russian Empire during 1904 and 1905 over rival imperial ambitions in Manchuria and the Korean empire.

The major theatres of military operations were located in Liaodong Peninsula and Mukden in Southern Manchuria, and the seas around Korea, Japan, and the Yellow Sea. Romanov and the Russian Empyreal though Russia suffered several defeats, while emperor Nicholas II was convinced that Russia could win if it fought on.

Really he chose to remain engaged in the war and was waiting to see the outcomes of certain key Naval battles, but after the hope of Victory, put down, he continued the war only to preserve the dignity of Russia by turning away a" Humiliating Peace".

So, Russia ignored Japan's willingness early to agree an "armistice" this agreement to be at least for stop fighting for one certain time or the end of the war and rejected ide to bring this case to the permanent Court of Arbitration at Hague.

This treaty of Portsmouth 5 September 1905 mediated by President of the U.S.A. MR. Theodore Roosevelt.

This complete and big victory of the Japanese surprised international observers and transformed the balance of power in both of Asia and Eastern Europe.

This victory made that Japan to emerge as a great power and Russia to decline in prestige and influence in Eastern Europe.

But let' see now what was cause of this very terrible war that created unbelievable lost of so many lives of people and weapon of military. First cause of this war was failed diplomacy by Russia to answer to negotiation of Japan empire.

During 1890s and 1900 was emerged one propaganda by German Government and German Emperor Wilhelm II (r.1888 – 1918) of "Yellow Peril" that he often wrote to his cousin Emperor Nicholas II of Russia he was praising him like saviour of "The White Race" and urging Russia forward to Asia.

German Emperor Wilhelm II since November 1894 was writing letter about defender of Europe by, "Yellow Peril" to his cousin and he made specific phrase to assure and tell to Tsar, that God himself chose Russia to defend Europe from alleged Asian threat.

But what is "Yellow Peril" really:

He was explaining and was lifting his supposing based to some certain symptom on eastern Europe, that Japan is continuously moving customer.

Also, he ended his writing to his letter that "it is evident to every unbiased that Korea must and will be Russian" and China and Japan soon would and will be united against Europe so will be big force threat for Europe.

So, emperor of Germany Wilhelm II was convincing mind of emperor of Russia Nicholas II to fight Japan.

Some people at that time explaining that Nicholas II dragged intentionally with hope of reviving Russian nationalism. About this conflict with comment made by Nicholas to Kaiser Wilhelm of Germany that he said would be no war because he "did not wish it".

Really his answer did not reject the claim that Russia played aggressive role in east as it did. (as is done now really in current time in this war between Russia and Ukraine).

Really at that time Russia never believed that Japan will enter in war while named Japan people "Yellow Monkey" that can't fight with Russia that had superiority about Naval and Army. So, when Nicholas II Russian Emperor replied to German Emperor Wilhelm that he did not go on war, Wilhelm II wrote one telegram:

"You innocent Angel: This is language of innocent Angel but not that a White Tsar!"

Anyway, Tokyo believed that Russia was not serious about seeking peaceful, about the solution to this very important matter so Japan proposed one formula about territory on 13 January 1904 by which Manchuria would remain outside Japan's sphere of influence and, reciprocally, Korea outside Russia's. On 21 December 1903, the Tarō cabinet voted to go to war against Russia.

So, when diplomacy failed and Russia did not answer to negotiation before by Japan came the war, as always is happening like that in our earth planet

The Yellow Peril or Yellow Terror and the Yellow specter is a racial - metaphor that named the people of East Asia and South Asia as existential danger to western world.

This concept of yellow Peril is racial not national it is one fear with no, any specific source or danger from any one people or country but simple is one fear by people with faceless, nameless, so it like fear of something is going to happen unpleasant by those yellow people it is like inauspicious feelings nothing else.

So, this is feeling of xenophobia the yellow terror is oriental not – white other.

This is racial fantasy that is presented in the book "The Rising Tide of Color against White World -Supremacy (1920), by Lothrop Stoddard.

Number's game is showing again its power in magnificence way, that during this time "Twenty to thirty million Chinese, supported by half of dozen Japanese divisions, led by competent, intrepid (fearless, adventurous) Japanese officers full of hatred for Christianity – that is a vision of the future that cannot contemplate or to view or consider without concern, and it is impossible.

So this phenomenon it was a realization of the "Yellow Peril" that leader or Emperor of Europe were suspicious and happened for really.

This situation created some issue about different alliances that were created before.

So Wilhelm II German Emperor aggressively encouraged Russia's ambition in Asia, for only reason because during this time France was not so much supportive to Russia for expansion to Asia and why those two Russia and France were closest ally since 1894.

So the leader in Berlin of Germany believed that this situation of supporting by Germany of Russia will break up the Franko – Russian alliance and will lead to new alliance German - Russian alliance. At that time France's leader disapproved of Russia's Emperor, Nicholas's forwarded policy in Aisa.

The French Premier Maurice Rouvier (in office : May to December 1887) publicly declared that Franko – Russian alliance applied only in Europe not in Asia also he declared that France would remain neutral if Japan is attacked Russia {29} (Russian – Japanese war Wikipedia online}.

While at that time president of U.S.A. Theodore Roosevelt that will do mediation of Russian – Japan case, complain that Wilhelm's propaganda about "Yellow Peril" will be cause that strongly Germany to decide to enter in war with Japan to support Russia.

Also president of the U.S.A. Theodore Roosevelt wrote on July 24, 1905, to the British diplomat Cecil spring Rice that:

Wilhelm II Emperor of Germany made partial responsibility for the war as "he has done all he could to bring it about."

So the persistence of German Emperor Wilhelm II about "Yellow Peril" made Russian to be uninterested in compromise while believed that if Japan will attack Russia, Germany will help and will intervene in i[.{30} Russian – Japan war, Wikipedia. Online]

Repeated theme letters of German Emperor Wilhelm II to Nicholas II Russian Emperor was that "Holy Russia had been chose by the God to save "Entire White Race" from "Yellow Peril" and that Russia was

"entitled "to annex all of Korea Manchuria and northern China up to Beijing.{(40) Russian – Japan war, Wikipedia, online}.

Wilhelm II Emperor of Germany in persistence way tried to convince the mind of emperor of Russia Nicholas with his very talented writing of course that:

".....Wilhelm went on to assure Nicholas that once Russia had defeated Japan, this would be a deadly blow to British diplomacy, and that the two emperors, the self-proclaimed "Admiral of the Atlantic" and the "Admiral of the Pacific", would rule Eurasia together, making them able to challenge British sea power as the resources of Eurasia would make their empires immune to a British blockade, and thus allowing Germany and Russia to "divide up the best" of the British colonies in Asia between them."[[40]" Russian – Japan War. Wikipedia. online].

Bad management was done by Emperor of Russia Nicholas II that he decided to pursue bigger policy in Far East that led to military complications.

So, Russia took Port Arthur while get out of Baltic and made vulnerable herself to the others by the sea. Another mistake that was done by Russia was that entire divisions from Poland and European Russia have been sent to the Far East. Really this never will happen if those governments will be in agreement.

Nicholas had been prepared to compromise with Japan, but after receiving a letter from Wilhelm attacking him as a coward for his willingness to compromise with the Japanese (who, Wilhelm never ceasing reminding Nicholas, represented the "Yellow Peril") for the sake of peace, became more obstinate. {[41] Russian – Japan – war, Wikipedia, online}

Really what he wrote to Russian Tsar the Emperor of Germany Wilhelm II that convince his mind to enter in war.

"Wilhelm II, had written to Nicholas stating that the question of Russian interests in Manchuria and Korea was beside the point, saying instead it was a matter of Russia undertaking the protection and defense of the White Race, and with it, Christian civilization, against the Yellow Race.

And whatever the Japanese are determined to ensure the domination of the Yellow Race in East Asia, to put themselves at its head and organize and lead it into battle against the White Race.

That is the kernel of the situation, (cover or shell of the situation) and therefore there can be very little doubt about where the sympathies of all half-way intelligent Europeans should lie. England betrayed Europe's interests to America in a cowardly and shameful way over the Panama Canal question, so as to be left in 'peace' by the Yankees.

Will the 'Tsar' likewise betray the interests of the White Race to the Yellow as to be 'left in peace' and not embarrass the Hague tribunal too much? {[41] Russian – Japanese, war, Wikipedia, online}

But what happened at that time that Germany's Emperor Kaiser Wilhelm II, wrote letter to Russian Emperor Nicholas II?!

Japan issued a declaration of war on 8 February 1904. {[49] Russian – Japan war, Wikipedia, online}

However, three hours before Japan's declaration of war was received by the Russian government, and without warning, the Japanese Imperial Navy attacked the Russian Far East Fleet at Port Arthur. {[50] Russian – Japan war Wikipedia, online}

Tsar Nicholas II was stunned by news of the attack. He could not believe that Japan would commit an act of war without a formal declaration, and had been assured by his ministers that the Japanese would not fight.

When the attack came, according to Cecil Spring Rice, first secretary at the British Embassy, it left the Tsar "almost incredulous". {[51] Russian – Japan war, Wikipedia, online}

Russia declared war on Japan eight days later. {[52] Russian – Japan war Wikipedia, online}

Japan, in response, made reference to the Russian attack on Sweden in 1808 without declaration of war, although the requirement to mediate disputes between states before commencing hostilities was made international law in 1899, and again in 1907, with the Hague Conventions of 1899 and 1907. {[53][54][55] Russian – Japan War, Wikipedia, online}

During this time looked that changed the report and was coming like true the foresee of Emperor of Germany Keiser Wilhelm II about his hypothesis or theory about yellow race that will be together again Christianity and against white people.

The Qing Empire favored (Qing was Chinese dynasty at that time) the Japanese position and even offered military aid, but Japan declined it. However, Yuan Shikai, sent envoys to Japanese generals several times to deliver foodstuffs and alcoholic drinks.

Envoy, (every one of them) of Yuan Shikai (he was a minister plenipotentiary accredited to a foreign government who ranks between an ambassador and a minister resident. — called also envoy extraordinary, a person delegated to represent one government in its dealings with another, messenger, representative) was doing so much job by rule of his boss to help Japanese military at that time.

Who was Yuhan Shikai really that was influencing in his own?

Yuan Shikai (16 September 1859 – 6 June 1916) was a Chinese General military and government official who rose to power during the late Qing dynasty and eventually ended the Qing dynasty rule of China in 1912, later becoming the Emperor of China.

1- He first tried to save the dynasty with a number of modernization projects including bureaucratic, fiscal, judicial, educational, and other reforms.

2- He despite playing a key part in the failure of the Hundred Days' Reform.

3- He established the first modern army and a more efficient provincial government in North China during the last years of the Qing dynasty. before forcing the abdication of the Xuantong Emperor, the last monarch of the Qing dynasty in 1912.

4- Through negotiation, he became the first President of the Republic of China in 1912.{[1] Yuan Shikai, Wikipedia, online}

1- This army and bureaucratic control were the foundation of his autocratic rule.

2- He was frustrated in a short-lived attempt to restore hereditary monarchy in China, with himself as the Hongxian Emperor of China.

3- His death in 1916 shortly after his abdication led to the fragmentation of the Chinese political system and the end of the Beiyang, government as China's central authority.

4- Native Manchurians joined the war on both sides as hired troops during this time. {[56] Russian – Japanese war, Wikipedia, online}

What was result of the action of Emperor of Russia Nicholas II that was convinced by letters of Emperor of Germany Wilhelm ?!

1- Potential diplomatic resolution of territorial concerns between Japan and Russia failed

2- Historians have argued that this directly resulted from the actions of Emperor Nicholas II.

3- Crucially, Nicholas mismanaged his government.

4- Although certain scholars contend that the situation arose from the determination of Nicholas II to use the war against Japan to spark a revival in Russian patriotism, no historical evidence supports this claim.[42]

5- The Tsar's advisors did not support the war, foreseeing problems in transporting troops and supplies from European Russia to the East.[43]

6- The Tsar himself repeatedly delayed negotiations with the Japanese government as he believed that he was protected by God and the autocracy. [44]

The Japanese understanding of this can be seen in a telegram from Japanese minister of foreign affairs, Komura, to the minister to Russia, in which he stated:

Pre war negotiation. The 1890s and 1900s marked the height of the "Yellow Peril" propaganda by the German government, and the German Emperor Wilhelm II (r. 1888–1918) often wrote letters to his cousin Emperor Nicholas II of Russia, praising him as the "saviour of the white race" and urging Russia forward in Asia.[24][25]

1- From November 1894 onward, Wilhelm II had been writing letters praising Nicholas as Europe's defender from the "Yellow Peril", assuring the Tsar that God Himself had "chosen" Russia to defend Europe from the alleged Asian threat.[26]

2- On 1 November 1902 Wilhelm wrote to Nicholas that "certain symptoms in the East seem to show that Japan is becoming a rather restless customer" and "it is evident to every unbiased mind that Korea must and will be Russian".[24]

3- Wilhelm II ended his letter with the warning that Japan and China would soon unite against Europe, writing:

4- After courting the Japanese, Roosevelt decided to support the Tsar's refusal to pay indemnities, a move that policymakers in Tokyo interpreted as signifying that the United States had more than a passing interest in Asian affairs.

5- Russia recognized Korea as part of the Japanese sphere of influence[83] and agreed to evacuate Manchuria.

6- Japan would annex Korea in 1910 (Japan–Korea Treaty of 1910), with scant protest from other powers.[84]

7- From 1910 forward, the Japanese adopted a strategy of using the Korean Peninsula as a gateway to the Asian continent and making Korea's economy subordinate to Japanese economic interests.[83]

8- Russia also signed over its 25-year leasehold rights to Port Arthur, including the naval base and the peninsula around it, and ceded the southern half of Sakhalin Island to Japan.

9- Sakhalin would be taken back by the Soviet Union following the defeat of the Japanese in World War II.[85]

10- Roosevelt earned the Nobel Peace Prize for his effort.

11- George E. Mowry concludes that Roosevelt handled the arbitration well, doing an "excellent job of balancing Russian and Japanese power in the Orient, where the supremacy of either constituted a threat to growing America".[86]

12- As Japan had won every battle on land and sea and as the Japanese people did not understand that the costs of the war had pushed their nation to the verge of bankruptcy.

13- The Japanese public was enraged by the Treaty of Portsmouth as many Japanese had expected the war to end with Russia ceding the Russian Far East to Japan and for Russia to pay an indemnity.[87]

14- The United States was widely blamed in Japan for the Treaty of Portsmouth with Roosevelt having allegedly "cheated" Japan out of its rightful claims at the peace conference.

15- On 5 September 1905 the Hibiya incendiary incident - as the anti-American riots were euphemistically described - erupted in Tokyo and lasted for three days, forcing the government to declare martial law.[87]

(Martial Law: The exercise of government and control by military authorities over the civilian population of a designated territory. Martial law is an extreme and rare measure used to control society during war or periods of civil unrest or chaos.)

Casualties

But is showing up the Numbers' game for this war about tis casualties?!

1- The number of Japanese Army dead in combat or died of wounds is put at around 59,000 with around 27,000 additional casualties from disease, and between 6,000 and 12,000 wounded.

2- Estimates of Russian Army dead range from around 34,000 to around 53,000 men with a further 9,000–19,000 dying of disease and around 75,000 captured.

3- The total number of dead for both sides is generally stated as around 130,000 to 170,000.[88] China suffered 20,000 civilian deaths, and financially the loss amounted to over 69 million taels' worth of silver.

(Tael (pronunciation/ tei/ is a weight used in China and Asia of varying amount to 38 gram silver, but in China has fixed 50 gram silver (13/4 oz).

4- 'Due to the intercession or meeting of Russia, Germany and France, the Manchurian government paid Japan 300 million taels of silver to 'reclaim' Liaotung.

5- During the battle on the sea was done some action about transported thousands soldiers while some of them died after their ships went down.

6- Another bad phenomenon happened during this war on battle on the sea where many ships failed or refused to rescue soldiers that were shipwrecked they did not find consensus about what to do about them.

7- This led to the creation of the second Geneva Convention in 1906, which gave protection and care for shipwrecked soldiers in armed conflict.

Political Consequences.

1- This was the first major military victory in the modern era of an Asian power over a European nation.

2- Russia's defeat was met with shock in the West and across the Far East. Japan's prestige rose greatly as it came to be seen as a modern nation.

3- Concurrently, Russia lost virtually its entire Pacific and Baltic fleets, and also much international esteem. This was particularly true in the eyes of Germany and Austria-Hungary before World War I.

4- Russia was France's and Serbia's ally, and that loss of prestige had a significant effect on Germany's future when planning for war with France, and in supporting Austria-Hungary's war with Serbia.

5- In the absence of Russian competition, and with the distraction of European nations during World War I, combined with the Great Depression that followed to other situation about Japan became power.

6- The Japanese military began efforts to dominate China and the rest of Asia, which eventually led to the Second Sino-Japanese War and the Pacific War theatres of World War II.

To the western powers, Japan victory demonstrated the emergence of new regional Asian power. Opinion at that time was created and argued that this war had set the motion of a change of the Global world that now Japan was not regional power but really became the main Asian power. {(100) Russian – Japanese war Wikipedia online}

While U.S. and Australia were seeing about further diplomatic relationship and partnership but they seeing this changing of balance power by this war mixture with fear because they thought that "Yellow Peril" eventually shifting from China to Japan.

American figure like W.E.B. Du Bois and Lothrop Stoddards saw that victory like challenge to" Western Supremacy" {(102) Russian – Japanese war, Wikipedia, online).

This was Reflected to Australia where baron Christian Von Henrenfels interpreted the challenge in racial as well as cultural term arguing like "The Absolutely as Necessity of Radical Sexual Reform For Continuing of Existence of The Western Races of Man... Been Raised As Level Of Discussion To The Level of Scientifically Proven Fact."

To Stop Japanese Yellow Peril would require drastic changes to society and sexuality in the West. {(103

Certainly, the Japanese success increased self – confidence to Anti-Colonialist Nationalists to colonized Asian countries -Vietnamese, Indonesians, Indians, Philippians and those in declining countries like the Ottoman Empire and Persia in immediate danger of being absorbed by western Power. {(104) (105)

It also encouraged the Chinese who despite having been at war with Japanese only one a decade before still considered Westerns the great threat.

As Sun Yat- Sen commented"

"We, regarded Russian Defeat by Japan as defeat the West by the East. We regarded the Japanese victory as our own victory" {(106)

But who really is Sun Yat – Sen?!

Sun Yat -Sen it was stateman, physician, politician, political philosopher, that served as first provisional president of Republic of China and first leader of Kuomintang, Nationalist party of China also he is called "Father of the Nation" of the Republic of China and Forerunner of Revolution of the people of the Republic of China, for his instrumental role in overthrow of Qing Dynasty during Xinhai Revolution.

Even in Far- off Tibet the war was subject of conversation between Sven Hedin when he visited Panchen Lama in Tibet in February 1907. (107)

But really who was Sven Hedin?!

Sven Hedin was Swedish geographer, topographer, explorer, photographer, travel writer and illustrator, he was not Nationalist Socialist but he was Monarchist. (February 19, 1865 - November 26, 1952)

But who really is Panchen Lama?!

The Panchen Lama, is a tulku of the Gelug school of Tibetan Buddhism. Panchen Lama is one of the most important figures in the Gelug tradition, with its spiritual authority second only to Dalai Lama. Along with the council of high lamas, he is in charge of seeking out the next Dalai Lama. "Panchen" is a portmanteau of "Pandita" and "Chenpo", meaning "Great scholar".

While for Jawaharlal Nehru, then only an aspiring politician in British India, "Japan's victory lessened (reduce, minimize, decrease) the feeling of inferiority from which most of us suffered".

But who is Jawaharlal Nehru?!

Jawaharlal Nehru with nickname Pandit (Hindi: "Pundit" means teacher) born November 14, 1889, Allahabad India - died May 27, 1964 New Dehli) was an Indian politician, anti-colonial nationalist, secular humanist, social democrat, diplomat, journalist and author also first prime minister of independent India during 1947 – 1964, who established parliamentary Government and became noted for his neutralist (nonaligned) policies in foreign affairs.

Jawaharlal Nehru has daughter Indira Gandhi.

Indira Gandhi politician third prime minister of India, also first female prime minister of India.

A great European power been defeated; thus Asia could still defeat Europe as it has done in the past (108) and in the Ottoman Empire too, the "Committee of Union and Progress" embraced Japan as a role model. [(109) Russian – Japan war Wikipedia, online}

The humiliating loss in the 1904-1905 Russo Japanese War led to 1905 Russian Revolution; a long brewing discontent with the Russian social and political system. Tsar Nicholas II was thus forced to consider the transformation of the Russian government from an autocracy into a constitutional monarchy. However little changed on the ground and the resentment towards the ruling continued to rise.

Russia's poor performance in the Great War acted as a catalyst in quickly deteriorating the situation. Russia suffered heavy losses in men and territory and the social situation led to the Russian Revolutions of 1917. This ended the 300 year rule of the Romanovs with the rise of the Bolsheviks and a communist regime in Russia. The Romanov family was massacred in the process.

HAPSBURGS OF AUSTRIA-HUNGARY

In the age of rising nationalism, Austria Hungary was struggling with a large ethnic population, especially the Slav nationalism in the Balkans. The problem would in fact lead to the assassination of Austro–Hungarian heir apparent Franz Ferdinand by a Bosnian Serb, an event that caused Austria Hungary to start the First World War.

The Austro - Hungarian Empire completely ceased to exist as the War ended in the defeat of the Central Powers. Centuries of Hapsburg rule in central Europe ended with their exile. Moreover, Austria and Hungary were separated and reduced to small states surrounded by new and often less than friendly countries.

HOHENZOLLERN AND IMPERIAL GERMANY

As the war ended with the defeat of the Central powers, Germany was blamed for the entire conflict. The Hohenzollern dynasty, which had been the ruling house of Prussia since 1415 AD and that of Imperial Germany since 1871, lost both their sovereignty in 1918.

A wave of Marxist agitations spread across the falling empire, which were later suppressed by returning war veterans. Germany lost its colonies; large portions of territory to France and Poland;

and was left humiliated in the Treaty of Versailles. Kaiser Wilhelm II went into exile in Netherlands where he remained till his last.

THE OTTOMAN EMPIRE

With the death of Sultan Mehmed V in 1918, Sultan Mehmed VI presided over the dissolution of the Ottoman Empire under the Severes Treaty. The Arabic lands were divided among the British and the French and the Ottoman Empire was left to almost a fifth of the size of modern day Turkey.

This led to a national revolt under Mustafa Kemal Ataturk, against both Ottoman Empire and the Allies. The five year, struggle known as the Turkish War of Independence led to the Treaty of Lausanne in 1923 that superseded the Severes Treaty and established the Republic of Turkey. The monarchy was abolished and the last Sultan was exiled from Constantinople.

#5 RISE OF NEW NATION STATES

Though ethnic nationalism was on a rise for decades before WW1, the powerful and age old empires had the strength and resources to keep it in check. The Great War depleted the power of monarchs and as their Empires collapsed, new nations were born and were now able to survive in the new world order.

Austria-Hungary was split into Austria and Hungary and other independent states emerged from its territory, like Czechoslovakia and Yugoslavia. Russia and Germany gave land to Poland among other countries.

Lithuania, Latvia and Estonia gained independence from Russia along with Finland. Armenia, Georgia and Azerbaijan were established as independent states in the Caucasus region but were over time absorbed into the Soviet Union.

With the collapse of the Ottoman Empire; Syria, Jordan, Iraq and Palestine were declared "mandates" under the League of Nations. France essentially took control of Syria and Britain took control over the remaining three mandates. What was left of the Ottoman Empire became Turkey after the Turkish War of Independence.

#6 MILLIONS OF WOMEN ENTER THE WORKFORCE.

The First World War was a pivotal moment in the impact of women's role in society. As warring countries mobilized for war and later entered a state of 'total war', millions of men entered the military and armed services.

The drain in the labor pool caused by the vacating servicemen created a vacuum that could only be filled by the women.

This meant that significant number of women entered into jobs, even in areas where they were traditionally thought to be incompetent like heavy industry, munitions and police work.

This was mostly viewed as a temporary situation and women were frequently forced out of jobs as the soldiers returned. But during the years between 1914 and 1918, women learned skills and independence, which would have long term benefits and consequences for those societies. Some women publicly embraced this new access to traditionally male occupations and were determined not to relinquish them when the war was over. There were others not keen on the new challenges and eager for a return to pre-war conditions. But the door had now opened and the beginning of a social change had begun.

#7 EMERGENCE OF UNITED STATES AS A WORLD POWER.

With its vast resources and the advent of the second industrial revolution, America was a rising economic power in the decades preceding WWI. However Europe and its colonial empires had been for a few centuries the nerve center in the world.

The Great War and particularly the year 1917, marked a turning point in world politics, which would come a full circle in the coming decades and in the aftermath of the Second World War.

As war broke out in 1914 and prolonged, it began severely disrupting the European economies, allowing the United States to become the world's leading creditor and industrial power.

This became apparent in 1916 when European countries, especially Britain, placed larger and larger war orders with the U.S. Britain and France paid for these purchases by floating larger and larger bond issues to American buyers, denominated in dollars.

American President Woodrow Wilson had ensured that U.S. stayed neutral in the war; and his policy was partly responsible for his reelection in 1916. However, in the beginning of 1917 as Russia withdrew from the war, America's financial and political interests prompted it to enter the war on the side of the Allies.

A German general staff had perhaps rightly appraised American military strength as being somewhere "between Belgium and Portugal" A country with untapped military potential transformed with speed, turning into a large scale, fighting force towards the end of the war. Its entry thus tilted the balance in the favor of the Allies in 1918. Consequently, the United States became one of the major powers in the world.

#8 FAMINES AND DISEASES.

Famines and diseases were common and flourished in the chaotic wartime conditions. A louse borne typhus epidemic claimed the life of 200,000 in Serbia in 1914. As Allied blockades suffocated its enemies another 200,000 deaths occurred in the Great Famine of Mount Lebanon (1915-1918) and 750,000 German civilians died from starvation.

In Russia, the devastation caused by the War resulted in the 1921 famine killing anywhere between 5 to 10 million people and leaving 4.5 to 7 million homeless children. 3 million more died of typhus and 3.5 million of malaria.

The most devastating was the worldwide influenza pandemic, also known as the Spanish Flu. It broke out in 1918, killing more people than the war itself. With death count at somewhere between 20 and 40 million people, it has been cited as the most devastating epidemic in recorded world history.

So, the Numbers' game is showing itself so powerful with those very huge unbelievable numbers of tragedy of people in our Earth planet. Really so powerful is this Numbers' game about life of people, about their losing life unbelievable with million all these big numbers because of some very few people with very hot - crackbrain mind.

Those, situation can happen and in current time by this few kind of people that are so much danger for society. This is one big lesson of the World War I, that people must think so much before they to elect their leader in their country so to eliminate by the big disaster for their country and others countries around the world.

#9 TREAT OF VERSAILLE.

It was treat of peace that ended the war between Germany and allied powers after World War I. it was signed in Paris June 28, 1919 in Versailles, Paris five years after assassination of Archduke Franz Ferdinand in Sarajevo of Bosnje – Hercegovine.

The treat was to harsh in Germans that, was designed to humiliate and defeat enemy. This created seeds for future conflict of Germany with others country because with this treat Germany was required to accept the blame for all the loss and destruction caused during this world war!

This article 231 (as we see that numbers are powerful everywhere in every situation about every country and about every phenomenon that is happening in our Earth plane) was named "War Guilt Clause"

This article 231 made that Germany to know sovereignty of its former colonies and 13 % of its territory was taken away those territory came under control of allies in the League of Nation mandates.

What is mor interesting that this article and this treat signed was bringing in future big conflict and made the leader of Nazi of Germany Adolf Hitler to sing the document of occupied or France when a new government surrendered under Marshall Philipe Petain

And German forces occupied most of the country in same place in same path of forest with his mind to put again high the pride of Germany during the World War II. But the resistance of French people continued their fighting to sabotage this agreement or this action.

A minority of the French forces escaped abroad and continued to fight under General Charles de Gaulle and Free France. While the French resistance did so many sabotage operations inside German Occupied France.

In 1944 invasion of Normandy did so many sabotages about trains ammunition depots and fought Germans. After that the 2nd SS Panzer Division Das Reich which came under attacks and sabotage on their way across Normandy they created one massacre in Oradour – Glane while killed 642 of its habitants

#10 TEHCHNOLOGY ADVANCES.

This war that were involved more than 100 nations brought technology advances. Horses were not effective so created aircraft and tanks, with research, of chemistry discovered poison gas, with water they created submarine, because of so many wounded people they created extra rays, antiseptic, surface surgery drug and so many others medical supplies.

As many as 8.5 million soldiers and some 13 million civilians died during World War I. Four imperial dynasties collapsed as a result of the war: the Habsburgs of Austria-Hungary, the Hohenzollerns of Germany, the sultanate of the Ottoman Empire, and the Romanovs of Russia. The mass movement of soldiers and refugees helped spread one of most developed advance technology.

One of the most significant impacts of World War One was huge advances in technology, which would transform the way that people all around the world travelled and communicated.

World War I or the First World War, often abbreviated as WWI or WW1, was a global war originating in Europe that lasted from 28 July 1914 to 11 November 1918. Also known as the Great War or "the war to end all wars", it led to the mobilization of more than 70 million military personnel, including 60 million Europeans, making it one of the largest wars in history.

During the World War I, involved more than 100 nations.

Farmers in France, Germany, and Belgium are still at risk of becoming casualties due to the amount of munitions launched during World War I. When they plow their fields, they're still dredging up tons of unexploded weaponry, and sometimes the bombs go off.

By exposing the citizen armies of Europe to prolonged and extreme danger, World War One generated psychological casualties on an industrial scale. This, in turn, created a military crisis that drew doctors from a diverse range of specialties into the field of mental health; never before had so much attention been focused on a single psychiatric disorder.

The logistical demands of the war caused even greater damage. Wood was needed to support trenches, make paper, and as a construction material for all manner of items. The period of the First World War caused a timber crisis in Britain, with around half of its own productive forests being cut down, and forests in their colonies across the world also cut down at an alarming rate.

Before its entry into World War I, the United States of America was a nation of untapped military potential and growing economic might. But the war changed the United States in two important ways:

1- The country's military was turned into a large-scale fighting force with the intense experience of modern war, a force that was clearly equal to that of the old Great Powers;

2- ..and the balance of economic power began to shift from the drained nations of Europe to America.

In fact, America's entry into the First World War – which marks the beginning of the United State's history as a major power" and the end of the Monroe Doctrine – was "The result of its international moral responsibilities", which was much more in consonance with the county's political discourse and international identity.

What is the Monroe Doctrine?

This is doctrine of president of the U.S.A. James Monroe that first the doctrine articulated at December 2, 1823 to The State of Union Address in Congress.

But who was James Monroe?

American politician, 5th president of the United States (in office from 1817 to 1825)

James Monroe was an American statesman, lawyer, diplomat and Founding Father who served as the 5th president of the United States from 1817.

President Monroe was warning the European states or nations that the U.S.A. will not allow further colonization or puppet monarchs

The Monroe Doctrine was a United States foreign policy position that opposed European colonialism in the Western Hemisphere. It held that any intervention in the political affairs of the Americas by foreign powers was a potentially hostile act against the U.S. The doctrine was central to U.S. foreign policy for much of the 19th and early 20th centuries. {Monroe Doctrine, {Monroe Doctrine. Wikipedia.}

That time so many influential people there were discussing about situation of the U.S.A. and about its military. One of them was and influential person Alfred Mahan, that in that time he said that merchant shipping requires the protection by Naval forces.

The Fundamental Requirements of a Navy are realized in the existence of an adequate merchant marine base.

Mahan said that certain political circumstances might lead a nation to the development of Naval strength in the absence of proportionate mercantile interests. Mahan was discussing about the Naval and nonnaval portions of the nation's overall maritime posture. He was said that are some countries like Norway and Greece that were developing merchant fleets without proportionate Naval protection.

But the Idea of Alfred Mahan was provided for him several hundred years earlier by Sir Walter Raleigh:

"He who rules the sea control the commerce of the World and thus the riches of the world and finally the world itself"

Another idea of Alfred Mahan was about strategy necessity for out ward of the U.S.A. – expansion, it was that :

"To define the principal conditions affecting a nation's ability and will project its influence across the sea"

"The principal conditions affecting the Sea power of nations, viz, Geographical position, Physical Conformation, Extent of Territory, Character of Population and Character of the Government".

(Concepts of Sea Power – Admiral Alfred Thayer Mahan; By Cmde V Venugopal Menon (Retd.)

However, while an exact end date is a matter of debate, it's obvious the end of the Great Depression correlates somewhat with the beginning of the war, leading many to believe WWII must have ended the Great Depression and triggered the economic recovery of the United States.

Seven consequences of the WWI

1- Death and destruction.

During the course of the war, 8 million soldiers died in total and 9 million civilians. In addition, the bombings destroyed 300,000 houses, 6000 factories, 1000 miles of train lines and 112 coal mines. In military terms, 12 million tons of ships were sunk.

These numbers increase if we consider the tremendous physical and psychological damage suffered by millions of people, including soldiers and civilians, during the war.

Even within these data we can consider that the terms on which Germany had to surrender were those that provoked the uprising of Hitler a few years later. Many historians consider that the war never ended, that is, it was only a long cease-fire until the beginning of the next.

2- Economic consequences

The war was a significant economic cost to the nations that participated in it. Germany and Britain spent about 60 percent of what their economy produced, having to raise taxes and borrow money from citizens.

Money was also printed to buy weapons and other inputs needed for battles, which contributed to the generation of inflation.

The war also generated trade restrictions, which were exacerbated by exaggerated protectionist policies adopted by countries. This generated a globalized breakdown of the world economic system, with disastrous consequences such as the Great Depression in 1929.

3- Appearance of new ideological currents

With the collapse of Russia under the pressure of war, the revolutionary socialists increased their power, making communist ideology an important force within Europe.

Although the global revolution that Lenin expected never arrived, the presence of a great communist nation in Europe like Russia, with a marked authoritarianism, changed the balance between Asia and Europe.

At first, Germany leaned toward Russia, but later formed its own new social democracy.

4- The end of the monarchies

World War I ended four major monarchies: that of Tsar Nicholas II in Russia, after which the World War I, brought communism, The reign of the Kaiser Wilhelm of Germany, the monarchy of Emperor Charles of Austria and the reign of the Sultan of the Ottoman Empire.

5- Emergence of new countries

From the old empires emerged new countries, for example, the Austro-Hungarian Empire that was divided in a number of independent states. Russia and Germany turned over land to Poland.

Thus the countries of the Middle East were under the control of Britain and France, while what was left of the Ottoman Empire became Turkey.

6- Social Effects

World War I generated major social changes, birth rates abruptly fell by the death of millions of young men. In addition to this, many citizens lost their homes and had to flee to other countries.

The role of women also changed, as they had to replace men in offices and industries. In this line, the rights of women, such as the right to vote, began to increase.

High social classes ceased to play such a dominant role in society as the middle and lower classes began to claim their rights after the war.

7- Lost a generation

Some historians consider that a complete generation was lost when so many young soldiers died. In addition, more than 7 million men were completely disabled to continue their lives normally due to the aftermath of the war.

Wounds to people were not only physical - mutilation, burns and facial damage - but also psychological, leaving a high cost in indirect consequences, much more than any previous war in history.

There was also a sense of disillusionment and distrust of political figures. It began a process of a bitter acceptance of reality, instead of the optimistic dreams that had existed previously.

Causes of World War I

Historians still do not reach consensus on what the real causes of World War I were. Although one antecedent to consider is the increasing power that Germany had that generated instability in the balance of powers between the nations of Europe.

As a consequence, this caused the following countries to form military alliances:

The Triple Alliance: Germany, Austria and Italy.

The Triple Entente: France, Great Britain and Russia.

With this in mind, we can consider that the causes of the war were the following:

Nationalism: All countries sought to strengthen their own interests.

Imperialism: European nations were forming empires and they began to enter into conflict.

Alliances: The two most important alliances - the Triple Alliance and the Triple Entente - were created to prevent war. An alliance of this kind is currently considered to endanger only the lives of citizens in order to maintain their prestige.

Alliances: The two most important alliances - the Triple Alliance and the Triple Entente - were created to prevent war. An alliance of this kind is currently considered to endanger only the lives of citizens in order to maintain their prestige.

Militarism: Many countries thought that having large armies and powerful armies was fundamental.

However, the fact that he pulled the trigger for the outbreak of the First War was the assassination of the archduke Franz Ferdinand of Austria on June 28, 1914. Austria declared war on Serbia and the countries took their alliances to the conflict.

In August, Germany invaded France through Belgium, which began the trench war between the two countries. From then on, the war on the western front consisted of a deadly stagnation, where one side tried to defeat the other side.

It was in 1917 that the United States entered the conflict. Before their arrival, the Germans attacked in March 1918, but were repulsed in August of the same year, forcing them To sign the acquaintance Treaty of Versailles In November 1918 that ended the confrontation.

Consequences of Reparations

Germany had to pay £6,600 million in reparations, or payment for casualties and damage done during the war.

Next, the treaty targeted Germany's army and naval forces. They were forbidden to have any submarines or any kind of air force planes.

The Navy was all but demolished, the treaty stating Germany could have only 6 battleships, and the army could have no more than 100,000 men.

The Treaty of Versailles (signed in 1919) and the 1921 London Schedule of Payments required Germany to pay 132 billion gold marks (US$33 billion) in reparations to cover civilian damage caused during the war.

(References: life persona.com)

{The Horrid Economic Consequences of World War I - We Still Suffer From Them. Retrieved from Forbes.com.

> {The First World War. Retrieved from bbc.co.uk.
> Consequences of the war. Retrieved from english-online.at.
> Consequences of World War One. Retrieved from thoughtco.com.
> The Global Effect of World War I. Retrieved from gilderlehrman.org.
> Lessons and Consequences of World War I: Back to the future? Andrew Korubko. Retrieved from voltairenet.org.}
> {The Great War-Effects. Suzane Karpilovsky, Maria Fogel, Olivia Kob Elt. Retrieved from ibatpv.org.}

10 CAUSES AND CONSEQUENCES OF THE SECOND WORLD WAR

Between the Causes and consequences of World War II We find the violation of the Treaty of Versailles and the subsequent invasion of Poland by fascist Germany, as well as its subsequent overthrow and the creation of the United Nations.

World War II was a war of global scale that took place between 1939 and 1945, fought between the Allied countries and the Axis countries.

The Allies were made up of the United Kingdom, China, the United States, and the Soviet Union.

Among the countries of the Axis are the Empire of Japan, Fascist Italy and Nazi Germany. It is one of the most global wars in history, as it took action in 30 countries and involved more than 100 million people.

During the war, all the great powers of the planet used their military, economic, industrial, scientific and human resources in a strategic effort, thus changing the course of history in all these areas.

116

Among its attacks and consequences are the Holocaust and the explosion of atomic bombs in Hiroshima and Nagasaki.

But how are perception of Hitler that did all this tragic event during the World War II and specific with Holocaust most of them were Jewish and so many others European people from Poland, Romania, Italia etc.

J.T. MacCurdy refers to an earlier report in which he had spotted three such "morbid tendencies", classifying these as "Shamanism", "Epilepsy" and "Paranoia".

But really who was J.T. MacCurdy.

MacCurdy is a psychiatrist who wrote about morale. MacCurdy studied about "The Structure of Morale". More specifically, MacCurdy studied London's overall response to German bombings during World War II, wanting to know how Londoners managed to stay so calm during the eight-month bombardment.

Exactly what wrote Maccurdy:

{"The first, a term of MacCurdy seems to have borrowed from anthropology, referred to Hitler's hysteria and compulsion to feed off the energy of Nuremberg Rally-style audiences.

By now it was in decline, and his report refers to the "dull flatness of the delivery".

The other two tendencies were, however, developing. "Epilepsy" referred to Hitler's cold and ruthless streak, but also a tendency to lose heart when his ambitions failed.

MacCurdy thought the outcome of Operation Barbarossa, which had stalled the previous winter, had exposed this fatalism, and he wrote that Hitler's speech betrayed "a man who is seriously contemplating the possibility of utter defeat." Most alarming, however, was Hitler's growing paranoia.

By this, MacCurdy meant the Nazi leader's "Messiah complex", in which he believed he was leading a chosen people on a crusade against an Evil incarnate in the Jews. He felt that this was starting to become a dominant tendency in Hitler's mind.

The timing of such an analysis could not have been more prescient. Weeks before the speech, senior Nazis had set plans in motion for the Final Solution – an intensification of the mass extermination of Jews.

The paper notes an extension of the "Jew phobia" and says that Hitler now saw them not just as a threat to Germany, but as a "universal diabolical agency".

"Hitler is caught up in a web of religious delusions," MacCurdy concluded.

"The Jews are the incarnation of Evil, while he is the incarnation of the Spirit of Good. He is a god by whose sacrifice victory over Evil may be achieved. "}

An estimated total of 50-85 million deaths were accumulated, making World War II the bloodiest conflict in history.

The war cost $4 trillion dollar with current $

Also 5 million people died from Eastern Germany and Baltic states by murder, starvation and exposure while they being expelled from their home. People that fled the Soviet Union they repatriated and sentenced death.

After World War II Germany paid to Federal Government more than 102 billion marks, about $61, 8 billion at 1988 exchange rates, as reparation payment to Israel and Third Reich victims

Germany paid about 75 million marks ($49 million) by German firms in compensation to wartime forces laborer.

Causes of World War II

The Second World War was an extremely complicated event, which was triggered by multiple events from the end of World War I in 1918. Among these are:

1- Treaty of Versailles

At the end of World War I was signed the Treaty of Versailles proposed by the United States, where Germany had to assume responsibility for the war.

Colonies were abolished, the use of the air force and also had to pay an economic remuneration to the victorious countries.

This stripped Germany of its territory and destabilized its economy strongly, making its citizens not trust their rulers and their ability to lead the consequences.

2- Fascism and the National Socialist Party

In the early 1920s, the fascist party of Benito Mussolini ascended to power in Italy. This nation moved under the idea of nationalism, a form of government that imposed rigidity on the economy, industrial control and control of its citizens.

The empire of Japan was also strongly driven by nationalism and its promises of wealth and development.

This movement reached the north of Germany, where it was taken over by the union of workers and created the National Socialist party or Nazi Party, in which Adolf Hitler ascended to the power.

3- Failures in the Peace Treaty

The peace treaties seek to establish a just resolution, but the penalties imposed on Germany by the United States were seen as very severe; Nations such as Britain and France saw just that Hitler had protested.

The new Prime Minister of Great Britain, Neville Chamberlain, proposed new terms with Germany in the Treaty of Munich.

In this, he promised to yield to Hitler's demands to prevent a new war, but his actions were not enough.

4- Failed Intervention of the League of Nations

In 1919 the League of Nations was created. The plan was for all nations to unite, and if a problem arose, they would settle their differences with diplomacy and not with the use of military force.

But with the crisis of the decade of 1930 many countries stopped to trust in her. Nations like Japan and the USSR strengthened their military forces, because they did not trust in diplomacy, since the League did not have the support of all the countries, had no army at their disposal and did not act immediately.

5- Militarization of Germany and the invasion of Poland

From 1935, Hitler began to violate the Treaty of Versailles with the militarization of Germany and the annex of territories like Austria.

This was easy because the economic crisis further encouraged its citizens, who saw the treaty unfair from the beginning.

Just after signing the Munich Agreement with Neville Chamberlain, Hitler decides to invade Poland, thus violating any peace treaty and starting the armed conflict.

6- Consequences

The consequences of this massive event affected all the countries of the world, from the political, economic, social and even geographic reach.

7- Creation of the United Nations

After the fall of the failed League of Nations, the Allied countries formed the United Nations Organization in October 1945, at the end of the war. The UN would be stronger and would have more scope than its predecessor.

In 1948, the organization adopted the Universal Declaration of Human Rights. Since then it has been a body dedicated to maintaining the collective peace and security of nations

7- End of colonialism and imperialism

With the fall of the Japanese empire, fascist Italy and Nazi Germany, these nations became democracies. Due to the global consequences of the war, the vast empires ceased to exist and the state nations spread.

8- Economic crisis

As a result of an exorbitant spending on military power and resources, the warring countries were hit by a severe economic crisis. Germany, France and England filed for bankruptcy.

This in turn caused that France and England had to give up their colonies (like India or Algeria), thus creating multiple independent new nations that today are part of the denominated third world thanks to its history of economic and territorial despojo (Stolen territories).

9- Geopolitical changes in Europe

All Axis countries lost extensions of their territory to pay compensation to the Allies.

This caused a re-ordering of the world map. The USSR, for example, took countries from Eastern Europe and communism In these territories.

Germany also underwent changes and was separated into two nations: East Germany and West Germany; The first under a socialist government and the second, a democratic nation.

10- Emergence of the powers of the block: USA vs USSR

All Axis countries lost extensions of their territory to pay compensation to the Allies.

This caused a re-ordering of the world map. The USSR, for example, took countries from Eastern Europe and communism in these territories.

At the end of the war, the US and the USSR benefited because they did not suffer financial damage or damage to infrastructure and managed to increase their industrial power and thus become world powers.

This would initiate a new stage called the Cold War, where these two nations competed for decades in the political, economic, social, scientific and even sports. This rivalry would last almost 50 years.

The negative effects of this war are just way too many to recount as it brought out the worst in all of us.

Fatalities:

World War2 resulted in the death of nearly 75 million, and that's a rough estimate though when you take into account the result of those who died as a result of indirect effects of the war, like Famine, the total number could well cross 100 million.

An estimated total of 60–85 million people perished, or about 3% of the 1940 world population (est. 2.3 billion). Deaths directly caused by the war (including military and civilian fatalities) are estimated at 50–56 million, with an additional estimated 19–28 million deaths from war-related disease and famine.

TOTAL   [POPULATION   OF   THE   WORLD.   1/1/1939. 2,300,000,000[143]

MILITARY DEATHS FOR ALL CAUSES: 21,000.000 TO 25, 500.000

CIVILIAN DEATH BY MILITARY ACTIVITIES AND

CRIME AGAINST OF HUMANITY: 29,000.000 TO 30,500.000

CIVILIAN DEATH RELATED TO FAMINE DISEAS: 19,000.000 TO 28,000.000

TOTAL DEATHS: 70.000.000 TO 85,000.000

DEATHS OF POPULATION AS A% OF 1939 POPULATION : 6,900,000 to 7,400,000: 3.0 TO 3.7

AVERAGE DEATHS OF POPULATION AS A% OF 1939
POPULATION: 3.35

Country.	Population		
	1/1/1939	Military death,	Total Death.
Albania	1,073.000	3000.	30.200
Australia	6.968.000	39. 800	40.500
Austria	6.653.000	Including Germany	-
(Union with Germany)			
Belgium	8.387.000	12.000	88.000
Brazil.	40.289.000	1.000	2.000
Bulgaria.	6.458.000	8.500	21.500
Burma	16.119.000	2.600	252.600

(British colony).

Canada.	11.267.000	42.000	43.600
China.	517.568.000,	3.000.000- 3.700.000,	15.000.000 – 20.000.000
(1937- 1945)			
Cuba	4.235.000	-	100
Czechoslovakia.	14,612,000,	35.000- 46.000,	340.000 -355.000

(in postwar 1945–1992 borders)

Denmark.	3.795.000	-	6.000
Dutch East Indies.	69.435.000	11.500,	3.000.000 to 4.000.000
Egypt	16.492.000	1.100	1.100
Estonia.	1.134.000	34.000	83.000

(both in soviet and German-forces)

(within 1939 Borders),

Ethiopia.	17.700.000	15.000	100.000
Findland.	3.700.000	94.700	96.800
France,	41.680.000	210.000	600.000

(including colonies).

French Indochina.	24.660.000	-	1.000.000 to 2.200.000
Germany.	69.300.000	4.440.000	6.900.000 to 7.400.000 to 5.318.000,
Greece.	7.222.000	35.100	507.000 to 807.000
Guam	22.800	1000- 2000	1.000 to 2.000
Hungary.	9.129.000	200.000	464.000 to 864.000

(figures in 1938 borders not including territories annexed in 1938–41)

Countries	Population.1/1/1939.	Military Deaths.	Total deaths.
Iceland	118.900	-	200
India.	377.800.000	87.000,	2.200.000
to 3.087.000			
Iran	14.340.000	200	200
Iraq	3.698.000	500	700
Ireland	2.960.000	5.000	100

(Irish, volunteers included with UK Armed Forces.)

Italy.	44.394.000	319,200 to 341,000.	492.400 to 514.000.

(Italian nationals and c. 20,000 Africans conscripted by Italy)

Japan.	71.380.000 to 2.300.000	2.100.000 to 3.100.000	2.500.000
Korea.	24.326.000		483.000
(Japanese colony)		(Included with	to 533.000
		Japanese Military)	

Country	Population1/1/1939	Military Deaths.	Total deaths.
Latvia.	1.994.500	30.000	250.000

(In both Soviet and German Armies.) (Within 1939 borders)

Lithuania.	2.575.000	25.000	370.000

(In both Soviet and German Armies) (Within 1939 borders)

Luxeombourg.	290.000	1900	7.106

(Included German and Allied Military)

Malaya& Singapore	5.185.000	-	100.000
Malta	269.000	(Included with U.K)	1.500
Mexico	19.320.000	-	100
Mongolia	819.000	500	300
Nauru	3.400	-	500
Nepal	6.875.000	(Including with British Indian Army)	
Netherland.	8.729.000	6.700	210.000

Country	Population 1/11939	Military Deaths	Total Deaths
New Foundland	320.000	1.100	1.200

(Including with U.K. and Canada)

New Zealand.	1.629.000	11.700	11.700
Norway.	2.9450.000	2.000	10.200
Papa New Guinea.	1,292,000	-	15.000
Philipines.	16.303.000	57.000	557.000
Poland.	34.849.000	240.000	5.900.000
(Within 1939 borders, 6.000.000 including territories annexed by USSR)			
Portuguese Timor	480.000	-	40.000 to 70.000
Romania.	15.970.000	300.000	500.000
Ruanda Urundi	3.800.000	-	36.000 to 50.000
South Africa.	10.160.000	11.900	11.900
South seas mandate	127.000	-	10.000
(Japan's colony)			

Country	Population.1/11939	Military Deaths	Total Deaths
Soviet Union.	188.793.000	8.668.000	20.000.000
	to 11.400.000	to 27.000.000	

(Within 1946−91 borders including annexed territories)

Spain	25.637.000	(Included with Germany Army)	
Sweden	6.341.000	100	2.100
Switzerland	4.210.000	-	100
Thailand	15.023.000	5.600	7.600
Turkey	17.370.000	200	200
United Kingdom.	47.760.000	383.700	450.900

(Including Crown Colonies)

United states.	131.028.000	403.700	419.400
Yugoslavia.	15.490.000	300.000	1.027.000
	to 446.000	to 1700.000	
Other nations.	300.000.000		
Approximately,			
Total;	2.300.000.000	21.000.000,	75.000.000-85.000.000
	- 25.500.000,		

World Wide Casualties.

Battle Death.	15.0000.000
Battle Wounded.	25.000.000
Civilian Deaths.	45.000.000.

So the Number's Game it is showing it super power about those tragic numbers of deaths, where the first place of losing people is :

1- Soviet Union, (BRSS at that time), with 27.000.000 people,

2- China with 20.000.000 people.

3- Germany with 7.400.000 people.

4- Poland with 6.000.000 people.

5- Dutch East Indies with 4.000.000 people.

6- Japan with 3.100.000 people

7- India with 3.087.000 people

8- French Indochina with 2.200.000 people.

9- Yugoslavia with 1.700.000 people.

10- Hungary with 864.000 people

11- Greece with 807.000 people.

These numbers are showing for terrible tragedy that happened during the World War II, that people never to forget and never to be skeptical about any sign that is showing coming of the war.

So the Numbers' Game is showing its super power about those very different events of life of people and so all the time they can show like fact and their "Absolut Power "of those solid cold facts.

References

1- BBC (s.f.) World War Two. BBC Bitesize. Retrieved from bbc.co.uk.

2- English Online (s.f.) Results and Aftermath of World War II. English Online. Retrieved from english-online.at.

3- Essays, UK. (2013). What Were The Causes And Consequences Of WW II. UK Essays. Recovered from ukessays.com.

4- Hamner, C. (2012) Cause and Effect: The Outbreak of World War II. Teaching History. Retrieved from teachinghistory.org.

5- Hickman, K. (2017) World War II: Causes of Conflict. ToughtCo. Retrieved from thoughtco.com.

6- History Net (s.f.) World War II. History Net. Retrieved from historynet.com.

7- Kumar, S. (s.f.) Consequences of World War II. Dr. Susmit Kumar. Recovered from susmitkumar.net.

8- Visan, G. (2010) The End Game: The Consequences of World War II. Civitas Politics. Retrieved from civitaspolitics.org.

9- Your Article Library (2016) Top 11 Causes of 2nd World War. Your Article Library. Retrieved from yourarticlelibrary.com.

"At the end of the war, millions of people were dead and millions more homeless, the European economy had collapsed, and much of the European industrial infrastructure had been destroyed. The Soviet Union, too, had been heavily affected. In response, in 1947, U.S. Secretary of State George Marshall devised the "European Recovery Program", which became known as the Marshall Plan. Under the plan, during 1948–1952 the United States government allocated US$13 billion (US$151 billion in 2020 dollars) for the reconstruction of the affected countries of Western Europe."

The Soviet Union suffered enormous losses in the war against Germany. The Soviet population decreased by about 27 million during the war; of these, 8.7 million were combat deaths.

The 19 million non-combat deaths had a variety of causes: starvation in the siege of Leningrad; conditions in German prisons and concentration camps; mass shootings of civilians; harsh labor in German industry; famine and disease; conditions in Soviet camps;

and service in German or German-controlled military units fighting the Soviet Union. The population would not return to its pre-war level for 30 years.

Soviet ex-POWs (POW is a captivity in war not punishment but revenge but solely custody the only purpose is to prevent the prisoners of the war for not participation on further of the war) and civilians repatriated from abroad were suspected of having been Nazi collaborators, and 226,127 of them were sent to forced labor camps after scrutiny by Soviet intelligence, NKVD.

What is really NKVD?

The abbreviation of NKVD (formerly) People's Commissariat of Internal Affairs: The Soviet police and secret police from 1934 to 1943: the police from 1943 to 1946 0. This is definition of NKVD.

What was doing really NKVD?

NKVD in the U.S.S.R., as the government's secret-police organization (1917–30; 1934–46).

The NKVD undertook mass extrajudicial executions of citizens, and conceived, populated and administered the Gulag system of forced labor camps. Their agents were responsible for the repression of the wealthier peasantry.[8][9]

They oversaw the protection of Soviet borders and espionage (which included political assassinations), and enforced Soviet policy in communist movements and puppet governments in other countries,[10] most notably the repression and massacres in Poland.[11]

But what is for really "Extrajudicial Killing?!"

An extrajudicial killing (also known as extrajudicial execution or extralegal killing) [1] is the killing of a person by governmental authorities without the sanction of any judicial proceeding or legal process, other than in lawful military and police operations. They often target political, trade union, dissident, religious and social figures.

But what is for really, the term Gulag?!

The Gulag, "chief administration of the camps")[d][10][11][9] was the government agency in charge of the Soviet network of forced labor camps set up by order of Vladimir Lenin, reaching its peak during Joseph Stalin's rule from the 1930s to the early 1950s.[12]

English-language speakers also use the word gulag to refer to all forced-labor camps that existed in the Soviet Union, including camps that existed in the post-Lenin era.[13][14].

Same situation was in my native country Albania that so many people got the name Gulag (Kulak) by this agency because they were concentrated in camp labor or in village, but they were surveillance and they have so many restriction about daily activity compare with the others plus they never had the rights to vote.

I have worked like Agriculture specialist after I finished Agriculture University, that Government sent me to one Farm Gostime, Elbasan that were so many Gulags after they sent me in Shtepanje that were most of the people were Gulag. Village was so beautiful between Cerrik, of Elbasan and Gramsh close where is now Banja Hydrocentral that is for irrigation.

Beautiful relieve village was build in two sides of the main street, to the bottom of the hills, aside to field after was river. Beautiful nature.

People were so good, but they were most of them Gulags and persecuted. I never can forget one person over there that met me during my control close to his two floor like tower house maybe was close to 100 years building.

It was day of election in Albania and this good older man Murat Xhika, that was taller handsome but the time had created so many wrinkles during his suffering life said to me:

Agronome, (workers over there speaking only with title of profession), my grandfather and my father when he was young, they paid so much with golden coins to the commander of the military of Austro – Hungary that they never to damage our village until to go in border of Gramsh.

My family was patriot of this country and of our region but now we have not right to vote, so, I do not know when is coming day for me and most of all for my sons to vote in this village.

Really his sons were excellent students in high school but never has right to go to university.

He saw me with deep thinking but speech less, so after he said:

I know that is not in your power.

I replied: Right this matter it is not in my power it is by "Upper", but maybe one day you will vote who, knows I closed my conversation to make soft way of this discussing.

But what is really Political Assassination?

Assassination is the murder of a prominent or important person,[1] such as a head of state, head of government, politician, member of a royal family, or CEO.

An assassination may be prompted by political and military motives, or done for financial gain, to avenge a grievance, from a desire to acquire fame or notoriety, or because of a military, security, insurgent or secret police group's command to carry out the assassination.

Acts of assassination have been performed since ancient times. A person who carried out an assassination is called an assassin or hitman.

But what is for really "Policy soviet".

It is a vanguard party, organized hierarchically through "democratic centralism", would seize power "on behalf of the proletariat", and establish a one-party socialist state, which they call the "dictatorship of the proletariat".

The state would control the economy and means of production, suppress opposition, counter-revolution and the bourgeoisie, and promote collectivism, to pave the way for an eventual communist society that would be classless and stateless all it is to replace capitalism.[5][7][8][9][10][11]

Generally, their ideology opposes, anarchism, fascism, imperialism, and liberal democracy.

So definitely the NKVD (ProperNoun) it was the People's Commissariat for Internal Affairs the Soviet secret police, forerunner of the KGB.

{(5.7.8.9.10.11.12.13.14.) NKVD. Wikipedia online}

Many ex-POWs and young civilians were also conscripted to serve in the Red Army. Others worked in labor battalions to rebuild infrastructure destroyed during the war.

***The economy had been devastated. Roughly a quarter of the Soviet Union's capital resources were destroyed, and industrial and agricultural output in 1945 fell far short of pre-war levels.

To help rebuild the country, the Soviet government obtained limited credits from Britain and Sweden; it refused assistance offered by the United States under the Marshall Plan.

Instead, the Soviet Union coerced Soviet-occupied Central and Eastern Europe to supply machinery and raw materials. Germany and former Nazi satellites made reparations to the Soviet Union.

The reconstruction program emphasized heavy industry to the detriment of agriculture and consumer goods. By 1953, steel production was twice its 1940 level, but the production of many consumer goods and foodstuffs was lower than it had been in the late 1920s.

So, the Number's game gave so much big and unpredictable result about creating new allies and new map of territories.

After World War II - period most part s of the Europe, was dominated by the Soviet Union annexing, while all the countries invaded and annexed by the Red Army driving the Germans out of central and eastern Europe.

New states were allies at that time with the Soviets like Poland, Bulgaria, Hungary, Czechoslovakia, Romania, Albania, and East Germany.

Yugoslavia stood an independent Communist state allied but not aligned with the Soviet Union, while created the independent nature of the military victory of the Partisans of Josip Broz Tito during World War II in Yugoslavia.

The Allies established the Far Eastern Commission and allied council for Japan to administer their occupation of that country also those allies, also established allied control council about administrated occupied Germany. By the agreement of Potsdam conference, the Soviet Union occupied and annexed the strategic island of Sakhalin.

U.S. policy after World War II from April 1945 until to July 1947 had been that not to help Germany in rebuilding their nation but to put in minimum or painless about starvation.

This "industrial disarmament" plan after the World War II for Germany had been to destroy Germany's capability to do war against others country in future by complete or partial de – industrialization.

So, this the first plan – program that was designed in 1946, decided that Germany to destroy 1500 manufacturing plants that will send Germany's economy in 50 % down in same level that was in 1938.

Dismantling of West German industry ended in 1951. By 1950 equipment had been removed from 706 manufacturing plants, and steel production's capacity, was reduced by 7, 6 million tons.

When administrate of Truman of the U.S. together with Joint Chief of Staff and general Lucius ID. Clay and George Marshal when they saw situation in Europe, they accepted that recovery of Europe's economy could not forward without reconstruction of economy of Germany and recovery of industrial base that were before countries of Europe depended.

So, in July 1947, President Truman revoke or cancelled on "national ground "the directive that ordered and not allowed U.S occupation forces to take steps for rehabilitation of Germany's economy.

The new directive recognized and required about contributions and establish of the economy of Germany. From 1946 Germany got helping through the "GARIOA" program.

But what is really GARIOA?

Government Aid and Relief in Occupied Areas (GARIOA) was a program under which the United States after the 1945 end of World War II from 1946 onwards provided emergency aid to the occupied nations of Japan, Germany, and Austria. The aid was predominantly in the form of food to alleviate starvation in occupied area.

On June 5, 1946, was revoked the order about prohibiting of sending packages to individuals in Germany, because before the different organization were forbidden to send food over there (Germany).

Also the Red Cross was prohibiting to send food or visiting POW camps Germans inside Germany, but in autumn of 1945 after they approached to allies, was creating possibilities, to investigate camps in U.K and French's occupation zones of Germany.

Also Red cross was allowed on February 4, 1946, the U.S. occupation zone in Germany to visit and assist prisoners with very small quantity of food.

Definitely Red Cross petitioned successfully of improvement to happen about of living condition of German POW. (POW is a person who is held captive like prisoner by a belligerent power during or after armed conflict).

France

When France was liberated from German occupation started inside this country one new phenomenon that named itself" "epuration", "purge", and started for really suspected of Nazi collaborators. At that time by French resistance was starting operation of "Epuration Sauvage" or "wild purge" that really it was one extralegal manner.

What was really this action, by French resistance:

1- French women who had romantic liaisons with German soldier s were publicly humiliated ad had their head shave.

2- They have done so many executions that estimated to have killed about 10,000 people.

3- When the provisional French government of French republic established control, the "Epuration Legale" ("Legale Purge") began.

4- There were no International war crimes trials for French collaborators, who were tried in domestic courts.

5- Approximately 300,000 cases were investigated.

6- 120,000 people were given various sentences including 6,763 death sentences (of which only 791 were carried out).

7- Most convicts were given amnesty a few years later.

But what is really the term of theme is the "Epuration Sauvage", or the wild purge, during the period between the liberation of French territory and the establishment of a French civil government. It was a time of violence, when the French turned on themselves in an orgy of retribution. Over ten thousand people were executed without trial.

Italy!

The 1947, Treaty of Peace with Italy gave the end of the Italian colonial empire, along with other border revisions.

The 1947 Paris Peace Treaties compelled Italy to pay:

1- $360 million (US dollars at 1938 prices) in war reparations:

2- $125 million to Yugoslavia,

3- $105 million to Greece,

4- $100 million to the Soviet Union,

5- $25 million to Ethiopia and

6- $5 million to Albania.

In the 1946 Italian constitutional referendum the Italian monarchy was abolished, having been associated with the deprivations of the war and the Fascist rule, especially in the North.

Unlike in Germany and Japan, no war crimes tribunals were held against Italian military and political leaders, while the Italian resistance executed some of them (such as Mussolini) at the end of the war;

It was one phenomenon that happened in Italy about amnesty that named at that time "Togliatti" amnesty that took that name from communist party secretary Togliatti, really this amnesty pardoned all wartime common and political crimes in 1946.

If we are seeing what big impact is giving this "Number's Game in society about so many big phenomena, like is this Togliatti amnesty and why so many people saw tragic death. But there are some phenomena in current time that some people with dark mind are damaging so many people for some past stories, of course people never must forget and to be alert that never to happen again but not all the time to use like weapon all life to damage others while are hiding their really reason.

So, Italy government different from French resistance gave one big pardoned too those military or collaborate people or crime of the war.

The Italian government did that only to Unify Italian people, but this phenomenon never is going to happen in Albania, that are going 32 years and people never are stopping hate and fighting in wild way the other people after changed system from monism system to Democratic system. But this continuing with persistence way of this open war between persecuted people during former system and other people that were working normal in former system, this hate is sending nowhere Albanian people for really only is creating one long line way bold "hate" feeling by both sides that with new democracy they changed position or poles.

Austria:

The Federal State of Austria had been annexed by Germany in 1938 (Anschluss, this union was banned by the Treaty of Versailles). Austria (called Ostmark by the Germans) was separated from Germany and divided into four zones of occupation. With the Austrian State Treaty, these zones reunited in 1955 to become the Republic of Austria.

Japan:

Result of ending war about Japan.

1- After the war, the Allies rescinded Japanese pre-war annexations such as Manchuria, and Korea became militarily occupied by the United States in the south and by the Soviet Union in the north.

2- The Philippines and Guam were returned to the United States.

3- Burma, Malaya, and Singapore were returned to Britain and French Indo-China back to France.

4- The Dutch East Indies was turning back to the Dutch but was resisted leading to the Indonesian war for independence.

5- At the Yalta Conference, US President Franklin D. Roosevelt had secretly traded the Japanese Kurils and south Sakhalin to the Soviet Union in return for Soviet entry in the war with Japan.

6- The Soviet Union annexed the Kuril Islands, while with some provocation the Kuril Islands, Russia continues to occupy the islands.

7- Hundreds of thousands of Japanese were forced to relocate to the Japanese main islands.

8- Okinawa became a main US staging point. The US covered large areas of it with military bases and continued to occupy it until 1972, years after the end of the occupation of the main islands. The bases still remain.

9- To skirt the Geneva Convention, the Allies classified many Japanese soldiers as Japanese Surrendered Personnel instead of POWs and used them as forced labor until 1947.

10- The UK, France, and the Netherlands conscripted (recruited or mobilized) some Japanese troops to fight colonial resistances elsewhere in Asia.

11- General Douglas MacArthur established the International Military Tribunal for the Far East.

12- The Allies collected reparations (or restitution or compensation) of damage from Japan.

13- To further remove Japan as a potential future military threat, the Far Eastern Commission decided to de-industrialize Japan, with the goal of reducing Japanese standard of living to what prevailed (won victory) between 1930 and 1934.

14- In the end, the de-industrialization program in Japan was implemented (was decided by allies) (to a lesser degree than the one in Germany. Japan received emergency aid from GARIOA, as did Germany.

15- In early 1946, the Licensed Agencies for Relief in Asia were formed and permitted to supply Japanese with food and clothes.

16- In April 1948 the Johnston Committee Report recommended that the economy of Japan should be reconstructed due to the high cost to US taxpayers of continuous emergency aid.

17- Survivors of the atomic bombings of Hiroshima and Nagasaki, known as hibakusha (HIBAKUSHA) were ostracized (like gave cold shoulder or boycott, or reject) by Japanese society. Japan provided no special assistance to these people until 1952.

18- By the 65th anniversary of the bombings, total casualties from the initial attack and later deaths reached about 270,000 in Hiroshima[30] and 150,000 in Nagasaki.[31] About 230,000 hibakusha were still alive as of 2010,[30] and about 2,200 were suffering from radiation-caused illnesses as of 2007.[32] (casualties of WWII online)

Finland:

Result of this war to Finland!

1- In the Winter War of 1939–1940, the Soviet Union invaded neutral Finland and annexed some of its territory.

2- From 1941 until 1944, Finland aligned itself with Nazi Germany in a failed effort to regain lost territories from the Soviets.

3- Finland retained (kept its possession) its independence following the war but remained subject to Soviet-imposed constraints 9 WGS, {Wideband Global Satcom satellite form Block I of the space segment} showing its force) in its domestic affairs.

Baltic states:

Result of this war to Baltic states!

1- In 1940 the Soviet Union invaded and annexed the neutral Baltic states, Estonia, Latvia, and Lithuania.

2- In June 1941, the Soviet governments of the Baltic states carried out mass deportations of "enemies of the people"; as a result, many treated the invading Nazis as liberators when they invaded only a week later.

3- The Atlantic Charter promised self-determination to people deprived of it during the war.

4- The British Prime Minister, Winston Churchill, sat that time argued for a weaker interpretation of the Charter to permit the Soviet Union to continue to control the Baltic states.[33]

5- In March 1944 the U.S. accepted Churchill's view that the Atlantic Charter did not apply to the Baltic states

6- With the return of Soviet troops at the end of the war, the Forest Brothers mounted a guerrilla war. This continued until the mid-1950s. (34) (casualties of WWII Wikipedia online)

The Philipines:

Result of this war to Philipine!

1- An estimated one million military and civilian Filipinos were killed from all causes; of these 131,028 were listed as killed in seventy-two war crime events.

2- According to a United States analysis released years after the war, U.S. casualties were 10,380 dead and 36,550 wounded;

3- Japanese dead were 255,795.[35]

Population displacement

1- As a result of the new borders drawn by the victorious nations, large populations suddenly found themselves in hostile (unkind, unfriendly, like bitter situation for them) territory.

2- The Soviet Union took over areas formerly controlled by Germany, Finland, Poland, and Japan.

3- Poland lost the Kresy region (about half of its pre-War territory) and received most of Germany east of the Oder-Neisse line, including the industrial regions of Silesia.

4- The German state of the Saar was temporarily a protectorate of France but later returned to German administration.

5- As set forth at Potsdam, approximately 12 million people were expelled from Germany, including seven million from Germany proper, and three million from the Sudetenland.

6- During the war, the United States government interned (keep like hostage, inmate or prisoner) approximately 110,000 Japanese Americans and Japanese who lived along the Pacific coast of the United States in the wake of Imperial Japan's attack on Pearl Harbor.[36][37] (Casualties WWII Wikipedia online)

7- Canada interned approximately 22,000 Japanese Canadians, 14,000 of whom were born in Canada.

8- After the war, some internees chose to return to Japan, while most remained in North America.

Poland:

Result of this war in Poland!

1- The Soviet Union expelled at least 2 million Poles from the east of the new border approximating the Curzon Line. This estimate is uncertain as both the Polish Communist government and the Soviet government did not keep track of the number of expelled.

2- The number of Polish citizens inhabiting Polish borderlands (Kresy region) was about 13 million before World War II broke out according to official Polish statistics.

3- Polish citizens killed in the war that originated from the Polish border lands territory (killed by both German Nazi regime and the Soviet regime or expelled to distant parts of Siberia) were accounted as Russian, Ukrainian or Belarusian casualties of war in official Soviet historiography. This fact imposes additional difficulties in making the correct estimation of the number of Polish citizens forcibly transferred after the war.[38]

4- The border change also reversed the results of the 1919–1920 Polish-Soviet War.

5- Former Polish cities such as Lwów came under control of the Ukrainian Soviet Socialist Republic.

6- Additionally, the Soviet Union transferred more than two million people within their own borders; these included Germans, Finns, Crimean Tatars, and Chechens.

Really what magical power has Number's Game of life of nation of this earth planet. The power of numbers is giving big impact in every aspect of life of people.

HOW IS INFLUENCING THE NUMBER'S GAME ABOUT FOOD AND HOW IS INFLUENCING THE FOOD TOO, ALL AROUND THE WORLD!

Growing fast the number of populations on earth planet is one big issue, but dramatically increasing total global food production isn't the answer. To sustainably feed a planet of 9 billion, we must waste less food and curb per capita consumption of meat and dairy in those countries that already consume too much.

Thus, increasing food production requires expanding the agricultural frontier, a process that destroys biodiversity, interrupts hydrological cycles, and surrenders humanity to severe climatic change. This will hamstring (or make disable) humanity's ability to feed itself.

Global food production and land-use change have received less consideration in climate policy negotiations than they warrant. Halting deforestation is not some luxury that we can afford to trade, it has a huge and uncontrollable cost on its own.

Allowing deforestation to advance unchecked is the one way that we can be sure to end up with a planet so unhealthy that it can no longer meet the real needs of its human population. In this vein, climate negotiations, such as the upcoming COP21 in Paris, must strengthen measures to curb deforestation.

The "need" for extra food must come not from virgin forests slashed and burned for extra farmland, but rather from more efficient consumption habits.

What people can do:

Step One: Freeze Agriculture's Footprint

For most of history, whenever people have needed to produce more food, they have simply cut down forests or plowed grasslands to make more farms. People have already cleared an area roughly the size of South America to grow crops.

To raise livestock, they have taken over even more land, an area roughly the size of Africa. Agriculture's footprint has caused the loss of whole ecosystems around the globe, including the prairies of North America and the Atlantic's forest of Brazil, and tropical forests continue to be cleared at alarming rates.

But people can no longer afford to increase food production through agricultural expansion. Trading tropical forest for farmland is one of the most destructive things people do to the environment, and it is rarely done to benefit the 850 million people in the world who are still hungry.

Most of the land cleared for agriculture in the tropics does not contribute much to the world's food security but is instead used to produce cattle, soybeans for livestock, timber, and palm oil. Avoiding further deforestation must be a top priority.

Step Two: Grow More on Farms They Have Got

Starting in the 1960s, the green revolution increased yields in Asia and Latin America using better crop varieties and more fertilizer, irrigation, and machines—but with major environmental costs.

The world can now turn its attention to increasing yields on less productive farmlands—especially in Africa, Latin America, and eastern Europe—where there are "yield gaps" between current production levels and those possible with improved farming practices.

Using high-tech, precision farming systems, as well as approaches borrowed from organic farming, people could boost yields in these places several times over.

Step Three: Use Resources More Efficientl

People on earth planet already have ways to achieve high yields while also dramatically reducing the environmental impacts of conventional farming. The green revolution relied on the intensive—and unsustainable—use of water and fossil-fuel-based chemicals.

But commercial farming has started to find innovative ways to better target the application of fertilizers and pesticides by using computerized tractors equipped with advanced sensors and GPS.

Many growers apply customized blends of fertilizer tailored to their exact soil conditions, which helps minimize the runoff of chemicals into nearby waterways.

Organic farming can also greatly reduce the use of water and chemicals—by incorporating cover crops, mulches, (humus or top dressing) and compost to improve soil quality, conserve water, and build up nutrients.

Many farmers have also gotten smarter about water, replacing inefficient irrigation systems with more precise methods, like subsurface drip irrigation.

What is really drip irrigation?;

Drip irrigation is a micro – organism system that has potential to save water and nutrition, that allow water to drip slowly to roots of the plants either from above the soil surface or buried below the surface.

The goal is to place water directly into the root zone and to minimize evaporation.

So, drip irrigation is saving the water, but same times makes the water to reach the roots of the plant.

Advances in both conventional and organic farming can give us more "crop per drop" from our water and nutrients.

About green space's revolution that started to do one giant job about protecting planet only the Brazil nut trees – protected by national law – were left standing after farmers cleared this parcel of amazon rain forest to grow corn. Anyway, and why is done job about progressing of slowing deforestation, this northern state of Para saw a worrying 37 % spike over the past year.

Step Four: Shift Diets.

It would be far easier to feed nine billion people by 2050 if more of the crops people grew ended up in human stomachs. Today only 55 percent of the world's crop calories feed people directly; the rest are fed to livestock (about 36 percent) or turned into biofuels and industrial products (roughly 9 percent).

Though many of people consume meat, dairy, and eggs from animals raised on feedlots, only a fraction of the calories in feed given to livestock make their way into the meat and milk that we consume.

For every 100 calories of grain people feed animals, while people get only about 40 new calories of milk, 22 calories of eggs, 12 of chicken, 10 of pork, or 3 of beef.

Finding more efficient ways to grow meat and shifting to less meat-intensive diets—even just switching from grain-fed beef to meats like chicken, pork, or pasture-raised beef—could free up substantial amounts of food across the world.

Because people in developing countries are unlikely to eat less meat in the near future, given their newfound prosperity, we can first focus on countries that already have meat-rich diets. Curtailing or cutting or restraining the use of food crops for biofuels could also go a long way toward enhancing food availability.

Step Five: Reduce Waste

An estimated 25 percent of the world's food calories and up to 50 percent of total food weight are lost or wasted before they can be consumed.

In rich countries most of that waste occurs in homes, restaurants, or supermarkets. In poor countries food is often lost between the farmer and the market, due to unreliable storage and transportation.

Consumers in the developed world could reduce waste by taking such simple steps as serving smaller portions, eating leftovers, and encouraging cafeterias, restaurants, and supermarkets to develop waste-reducing measures.

Of all of the options for boosting food availability, tackling waste would be one of the most effective.

Taken together, these five steps could more than double the world's food supplies and dramatically cut the environmental impact of agriculture worldwide. But it won't be easy.

These solutions require a big shift in thinking. For most of our earth planet's history people have been blinded by the overzealous imperative of more, more, in agriculture clearing more land, growing more crops, using more resources.

Really people need to find a balance between producing more food and sustaining the planet for future generations.

This is a pivotal moment when people face unprecedented challenges to food security and the preservation of our global environment. The good news is that people already know what they have to do:

They just need to figure out how to do it. Addressing our global food challenges demands that all of us become more thoughtful about the food we put on our plates.

We need to make connections between our food and the farmers who grow it, and between our food and the land, watersheds, and climate that sustain us.

As we steer our grocery carts down the aisles of our supermarkets, the choices we make will help decide the future.

To frame this situation of the food of the world with some details of some big countries that are doing big impact of producing foods, some facts about that will leave everyone speech less.

By the statistic of "FAOSTAT", (Statistic Division of Food and Agriculture Organization of the United Nations. Initially observed were the commodities that had higher production in 2019, including milk, rice, beef, pork, and chicken.

For all those five commodities, is created one list of countries with highest production. Than, the lists were combined to create this overall ranking.

Top 10 Agricultural Producing Countries in the World.

It is not surprise, that China is one of the world's produces, importer and consumer of food products. While China's land is too mountainous or too arid for farming, the rich soil of the eastern and southern region are extremely productive. China also has one the world's largest workforce:

Some sources estimate that their workforces specifically for food production may as high as 315 million laborers

1- China:

The country is the largest producer of rice and pork, and is among the top 3 producers of milk, chicken and beef. In addition, China is the fourth largest exporter with 58.5 billion dollars in 2014. Compared to 2009, exports in 2014 represent a significant growth of 79.4%.

Thanks to its economic growth, China has halved the number of undernourished people since the 1980s. However, 150 million Chinese are still suffering from hunger, especially in rural areas. In addition, $ 32 billion of food is wasted annually, which is why China has developed programs for recycling leftover food.

2- U.S.A.

The United States is the second largest producer of pork and the largest producer of milk, chicken and beef. However, the country ranks 12th as a rice producer, that is why it didn't get the first position in the overall rankings. Expectedly, this country is the largest agricultural exporter, estimated at 110 billion dollars in 2014, making it ranked No.2 here.

3- BRAZIL

Brazil ranks among the top 5 countries for production of milk, pork, chicken and beef, and ranks ninth in rice production. The country has the ninth largest economy in the world, mainly for its agricultural production which contributes to much of the country's GDP. Brazil is also among the largest agricultural exporters.

4- INDIA

India is ranked the second in the world for milk and rice production. It also has high classification as producer of chicken and beef. With the export growth rate of 21.3%, India leads the list of countries with the highest export growth over the last decade. However, 30% of children in India are underweight.

5- RUSSIA

Russia, one of the world's leading countries for acres of land used for agricultural production, ranks among the largest producers of milk, beef and pork in the world.

After the West imposed economic sanctions on Russia because of its involvement in Ukraine's crises, President Vladimir Putin responded by banishing the import of food from the European Union, the United States and other countries that blamed him for the crisis in Ukraine.

6- FRANCE

France ranks among the top 10 countries producing milk and beef, and among the top 20 countries for chicken and pork production.

Also, it has the largest agricultural production in the European Union – 18.1% of the total European Union production comes from France, which became the fifth largest agricultural exporter in the world with an estimated export of 53.4 billion euros in 2014.

7- <u>MEXICO</u>

Mexico ranks high in the production of beef and chicken. It is also among the top 20 countries for the production of milk and pork. Despite these numbers, only a small portion of agricultural production represents the country's GDP. The country's agricultural exports in 2012 were estimated at more than 10 billion dollars, with annual crop output growth of 1.67%.

8- <u>JAPAN</u>

In 2012, Japan produced 10, 654,000tones, of rice and ranked 10th in the world for rice production. And it is also among the top 20 countries in production of milk, pork and chicken.

Expectedly, the Japanese consume mainly rice and fish, and eat less meat compared to citizens of the United States and the European Union. Japanese agriculture, fisheries and food exports reached a record in the last year, by an increase of 11.1% and was valued at 611.7 billion Japanese Yen.

9- <u>GERMANY</u>

Germany is the third largest producer of pork and also has a high milk and beef production. It is also the third largest agricultural exporter in the world, with a total export value of US $ 70.6 billion in 2014, an increase of 44.8% since 2009.

10- <u>TURKEY</u>

Turkey ranks ninth because of huge milk production, but also because of the high production of chicken meat. Also, it is among the top 20 countries in beef production. The country also has one of the highest export growth rates in the world as its agricultural exports have tripled over the last decade.

Top ten largest vegetable and fruits producer countries around the world.

1- China:

POINTS: 40

Finally, at the top of the list, is China, a nation that produced 160 million tons of fruits and 598 million tons of vegetables in 2016.

China exports tons of fruits and vegetables. More specifically, when it comes to fruits, China sells grapes, dates, figs, melons, nuts, apples, pears, dried apricots, prunes, apples, peaches and other similar fruits, frozen fruits, coconuts, citrus and more. In terms of vegetables,

China primary export lies in dried vegetables, whether whole, cut, sliced, broken or in powder, followed by onions, shallots, garlic, leeks, cabbages, cauliflowers, carrots, turnips and more, including dried leguminous vegetables, fresh or chilled produce.

It's important that people manage to keep changing climate in check unless want many of crops and fruits to disappear. Already, many are being affected by extreme weather conditions, higher temperatures and so on.

Hopefully, the outputs will continue growing, and we're not going to start seeing shortages as the population continues growing. This being said, it's also important that the world starts doing something about all the food that people are throwing away either because we don't consume it or because it doesn't look picture-perfect.

Either way, these have been the 10 largest fruit and vegetable producing countries in the world.

While to select the countries that are producing more fruits and vegetable around the world, people will see one very strange graphic of qualification:

***China is not only the most populated country in the world but when it comes to production of fresh vegetables and fruit China is the world's number 1!

Of the estimated (commercial) production of fresh vegetables in the world, China produces half. Of all the fruits, China produces 30%. From this enormous amount, only a small portion is exported.

Of 484 million tons of vegetables produced in 2012, only 4.4 million tons was exported.

That's less than one percent. Of the 220 million tons of fruit produced in 2012 only a mere 3 million tons were exported abroad. Despite these figures China remains high on the list of exporters.

With fresh vegetables China's export value is in fourth place and with fresh fruit export they are in 7th. Fourth fresh vegetable exporter and sixth for fresh fruit.

The production of both fresh fruit and vegetables in recent years has steadily increased. Exports have grown very slowly but since 2009 there was more capital (dollars!) creating stronger growth.

The increasingly expensive Yuan is another important part of the equation. The exchange rate of the Yuan compared to the Dollar and the Euro over the last 5 years has multiplied by 10.

Regional trade; only modest trade in EU (and The Netherlands).

Chinese export of fresh vegetables and fresh fruit is largely focused on countries in close proximity. Indonesia is the main buyer followed by (in 2012) Vietnam, Thailand, Malaysia, Japan, Russia, Hong Kong, the Philippines and South Korea. The United States comes in 10th behind Kazakhstan and Brazil, and the United Arab Emirates.

The Netherlands was the 14th recipient of Chinese fresh fruit & vegetables with, according to Chinese export statistics, an export value of more than $100 million dollars.

The CBS in 2012 recorded exports of fresh fruit & vegetables from China with a value of around 70 million Euros. The list of recipients of fresh fruit & vegetable from China is enormous, but other EU countries, except The Netherlands are not listed very high.

According to the Chinese export statistics conducted in 2012, England was worth 25 million dollars, Germany 12 million dollars and Spain and France, 2 million dollars each. According to Eurostat in 2012 there was 159 million Euros of fruit & vegetables exported from China.

Lots of garlic and apples exported Garlic is their most important export product. For all EU countries garlic is the main product imported from China but the 45,000 tons that went to EU in 2012, is nothing compared to the 400,000 exported to Indonesia.

In The Netherlands, garlic is the second import product following grapefruit imported from China. Chinese garlic export has otherwise not changed over recent years. \

Apples are China's second most important export product. Russia is the major importer of Chinese apples. After Russia, China's apples go to other countries in the region and hardly into Europe.

Soft citrus is the third export product and onions are fourth on the list. Over recent years, China has exported around 600 to 70,000 tons yearly.

This peaked in 2011 with 719,000 tons when there was a large demand for Chinese onions from Russia; more than 100,000 tons. Japan and Vietnam are normally the largest importers of Chinese onions. In the first half of this year there was a great demand from South Korea.

Also, Chinese onions mostly stay in the region. Other big Chinese export products are: carrots, pears, cabbage, tomato, kohlrabi, grapefruit, oranges, grapes and broccoli. It is quite surprising that The Netherlands is the largest importer of Chinese grapefruits.

In 2012 there was a total of 124,000 tons grapefruits exported of which 44,000 tons went to The Netherlands. The remainder went to Russia.

Strong import growth from Southern Hemisphere countries Chile, New Zealand, Peru, South Africa, Australia and Thailand are the main suppliers to China when it comes to fresh fruit and vegetables.

Products are mainly specific regional products such as durian, longan and mangosteen. The most eye catching is the rise of Chilean products on the Chinese market.

Last year 572 million dollars'worth of fresh fruit and vegetables were imported from Chile. In the first half of this year imports rose by 8%. There are a lot of sweet cherries, grapes, plums, apples and kiwi' s imported.

Vietnam also export dragon fruit. The Philippines is the supplier of bananas. Incidentally, during the first half of this year (according to Chinese import statistics) a third fewer bananas were imported to China.

The United States are also a major supplier of fresh fruit & vegetables to China. In 2012 they had an import value of 317 million dollars. In the first half of this year imports fell drastically; quantity -21% and value -16%. Grapes, oranges, and sweet cherries are the major import products, then there are apples, plums and lemons.

After the top 5 there was a gap and in 2012 New Zealand came six on the list. This is pretty much due to kiwi' s. Then follows Peru (mostly only grapes) and South Africa (grapes and oranges). Overall, bananas are the most important import product followed by dragon fruit, watermelon, longan, durian, grapes and mangosteen.

2- Hong Kong

Points: 38

Hong Kong, which is responsible for producing 158 million tons of fruits and 596 million tons of vegetables. This particular area is responsible for exporting loads of fruit and vegetables, including strawberries, raspberries, blackberries, apricots, cherries, peaches, grapes, citrus, apples, pears, dates, figs, coconuts and more, both fresh and dried.

This particular area is responsible for exporting loads of fruit and vegetables, including strawberries, raspberries, blackberries, apricots, cherries, peaches, grapes, citrus, apples, pears, dates, figs, coconuts and more, both fresh and dried.

When it comes to vegetables, Hong Kong exports large amounts of dried vegetables, whether whole, cut, sliced, broken, or in powder. Furthermore, they sell lettuce and chicory, steamed vegetables, onions, shallots, garlic, leeks, carrots, turnips, cabbage, cauliflower, and numerous types of roots.

3- India

Points: 36

On the third spot of the largest fruit and vegetable producing countries in the world, is India, a nation that produced 88 million tons of fruit in 2016, and a whopping 126.5 million tons of vegetables. India may be one of the largest producers of vegetables in the world, next to China, but it also exports quite a bit of what it makes.

Primarily, India exports coconuts and cashew nuts, as well as grapes, dates, figs, strawberries, raspberries, blackberries and other similar products, as well as bananas and other types of nuts, both fresh and dried or sweetened.

In terms of vegetables, India once more exports load of products. The largest group of vegetables it sells to other countries is made of onions, shallots, garlic and leeks, followed by dried leguminous vegetables, tomatoes, potatoes and more. The country also exports loads of dried or preserved vegetables.

4- U.S.A.

Points: 33

Next, is the United States of America, a country that produced nearly 26 million tons of fruit in 2016, and 36.5 million tons of vegetables.

The United States is one of the world's largest importers, but it also exports loads of things, including fruits. More specifically, the number one product the US exports from the fruit category is nuts, both fresh or dried, followed by grapes, apples, pears, citrus, strawberries, raspberries, blackberries, and others similar.

They also export apricots, cherries, peaches, bananas and more.

The US also exports vegetables, starting with cabbages, lettuce, tomatoes, onions, shallots, garlic, leeks, potatoes and more, both fresh or chilled, as well as steamed and frozen.

5- Mexico.

Points: 26

Up next on list of largest fruit and vegetable producing countries in the world, we have Mexico, a country that in 2016 produced 17.8 million tons of fruit and 14.2 million tons of vegetables. The country that lies south of the United States is one of the largest producers of fruits and vegetables in the world.

The country exports loads of fruits, including dates, figs, avocados, mangoes, guavas, strawberries, raspberries, blackberries and other similar fruits, as well nuts, melons, and citrus.

In terms of vegetables, Mexico exports loads of things, including tomatoes, cucumbers and gherkins, onions, garlic, leeks, cabbage, cauliflower and many others, both fresh and chilled, as well as frozen.

6-Turkey.

Points: 26.

In 2016, Turkey produced 14.2 million tons of fruits and 28.1 million tons of vegetables. Turkey's main fruit exports are various types of nuts, citrus fruits, grapes, apricots, prunes, apples, peaches, pears, as well as dates, figs, apricots, cherries, peaches, and nectarines, to name a few.

Turkey's main fruit exports are various types of nuts, citrus fruits, grapes, apricots, prunes, apples, peaches, pears, as well as dates, figs, apricots, cherries, peaches, and nectarines, to name a few.

In terms of vegetables, Turkey exports loads of leguminous vegetables, tomatoes, cucumbers, potatoes, onions, carrots, turnips, and more, both fresh or chilled, as well as dried whole, cut or powdered.

7- Brazil.

Points: 24

Beautiful Brazil is next. The country managed to produce 37.4 million tons fruits last year, as well as 11.7 million tons vegetables.

Some of the best fruits come from the here. The country's fruit exports focus on melons, dates, figs, avocados, guavas, mangos, and pineapples, as well as coconuts, Brazilian nuts and cashew, citrus fruits and grapes, plus, of course, bananas. No wonder it's in this list of the largest fruit and vegetable producing countries in the world.

When it comes to vegetables, Brazil exports loads of dried leguminous vegetables, roots and tubers of manioc, arrowroot, sweet potatoes and other similar produce, onions, garlic, leeks, carrots, turnips and more, both fresh, chilled or frozen.

8- Iran

Points:24

Iran is up next in this list of largest fruit and vegetable producing countries in the world, a country that produced 12.7 million tons of fruits and another 21.4 million tons of vegetables.

The country exports primarily multiple types of nuts, as well as grapes, dates, figs, fresh strawberries, raspberries, blackberries and other similar fruits, as well as melons, apples, and pears.

In terms of vegetables, Iran's largest exports in this category come from cucumbers and gherkins, cabbage, cauliflower, tomatoes, onions, garlic, leek and other similar vegetables, fresh, chilled or frozen.

9- Spain.

Points: 24

Next, is Spain, a nation that produced over 17.7 million tons of fruits and 14.1 million tons of vegetables. The European country produces loads of fresh fruit and vegetables and is known to export primarily citrus fruits, both fresh and dries, as well as strawberries, raspberries, blackberries and other similar fruits, as well as apricots, cherries, peaches, nectarines, plums and so on.

The European country produces loads of fresh fruit and vegetables and is known to export primarily citrus fruits, both fresh and dries, as well as strawberries, raspberries, blackberries and other similar fruits, as well as apricots, cherries, peaches, nectarines, plums and so on.

When it comes to vegetables, Spain is known for its exports of tomatoes, lettuce and chicory, cucumbers, onions, garlic, leeks and more, both fresh, chilled and frozen.

10- Egypt.

Points: 22

Egypt, a country that managed to produce over 11.6 million tons of fruits and 19.3 million tons of vegetables in 2014.

Egypt exports large quantities of citrus fruits, strawberries, raspberries, blackberries and other similar fruits, as well as grapes, dates, figs, and more, both fresh or dried.

When it comes to vegetables, Egypt's largest export group is onions, shallots, garlic, leeks and other similar vegetables, followed by potatoes, dried leguminous veggies, and tomatoes, both fresh and chilled or frozen. [For more info:Fruit & Vegetable Facts, Jan Kees Boon, fruitvegfacts@gmail.comwww.fruit, In terms of vegetables,}

EIGHT COUNTRIES THAT PRODUCES MORE GRAIN IN THE WORLD.

The largest grain producers in the world, such as Germany who makes a lot of Rye, or China, who is the largest producer of wheat in the world in 2016, are also important exporters of these particular grains. China is, of course, also the largest rice producing country.

There are eight countries around the world that are producing so much high quantity of different types of grain and why there are about 800 million people living with less food required to lead healthy lives according according, to UN World Food Program's Hunger Statistics.

That's 1 in 9 people on the planet. Still, things would have been much worse if it weren't for world's largest grain producers. Similar can be said for the countries that produce the most fish in the world. These countries too, do their fair share of global hunger relieving. Sadly, it's still far from enough. Before we begin, let's first define grain.

When mentioning grain, most people first think of wheat. While wheat certainly qualifies as a type of grain, it's far from only one.

Small, hard, dry seeds can be divided into cereals and legumes – being mostly interested in former.

A legume is a plant in the family Fabaceae, or the fruit or seed of such a plant. When used as a dry grain, the seed is also called a pulse.

Legumes are grown agriculturally, primarily for human consumption, for livestock forage and silage, and as soil-enhancing green manure.

Well-known legumes include beans, soybeans, peas, chickpeas, peanuts, lentils, lupins, mesquite, carob, tamarind, alfalfa, and clover.

Cereals themselves are further divided into warm and cool-season cereals, but they all belong to the grass (Poaceae) family.

1- Warm-season cereals include the likes of maize (corn) and millet,

2- Cool-season cereals are generally more widespread and include grains such as already mentioned wheat, barley, rice, rye, oats, etc. Of course, all legumes, soybeans, for instance, play an important role in global grain production and consumption diagrams.

China takes number one spot among these 8 countries that produce the most grain in the world. China is the world's biggest rice and wheat producer with 203,612,192 metric tons and Total

1- China:

Production: 557,677,392 metric tons

121,926,400 metric tons respectively. China also has a high maize production output, which amounts to 218,489,000 metric tons.

Finally, Chinese produce 11,950,500 metric tons of soybeans and 1,699,300 metric tons of barley.

2- U.S.A.

Total Production: 516,351,276 metric tons

The United States are by far the biggest maize producer in the world with yearly production coming to 353,699,441 metric tons. They are also world's leading producer of soybeans with 91,389,350 metric tons.

Finally, the United States produce solid 57,966,656 metric tons of wheat, 8,613,094 metric tons of rice and 4,682,735 metric tons of barley.

3- India:

Total Production: 289,698,000 metric tonnes

One of the largest countries in the world and the second largest country by population simply has to produce an abundance of food. India is world's second biggest rice producer with 159,200,000 metric tons a year.

They are also the second largest wheat producers with 93,510,000 metric tons. Maize production comes to 23,290,000 metric tons; soybeans come to 11,948,000 metric tons and India produces 1,750,000 metric tons of barley as well.

4- Brazil:

Total Production: 179,849,353 metric tons

Brazil is the second biggest soybean producer in the world with production of 81,724,477 metric tons a year. Maize follows close by with 80,273,172 metric tons, then comes rice with 11,782,549 metric tons and wheat with 5,738,473 metric tons. Finally, the largest South American country produces 330,682 metric tons of barley.

5- Argentina;

Total Production: 96,882,360 metric tonnes

Argentinian grain production mostly consists of soybeans and maize, which amount to 49,306,200 metric tons and 32,119,211 metric tons respectively. Next in line is wheat with the total yearly production of 9,188,339 metric tons. Barley and rice sit at the bottom with the production of 4,705,160 metric tons and 1,563,450 metric tons respectively.

6- Indonesia:

Total Production: 89,791,565 metric tons,

7- Russia;

Total Production: 81,685,645 metric tons

The Russian Federation has somewhat larger production output than Canada, but follows a similar pattern. Most of the Russian grain production falls on wheat with 52,090,796 metric tons. Barley comes second with 15,388,704 metric tons and maize is third with 11,634,943 metric tons. Finally, Russians produce 1,636,259 metric tons of soybeans and even 934,943 metric tons of rice.

8- <u>Canada:</u>

<u>Total Production: 67,319,400 metric tonnes</u>

Canada produces all considered types of grain, excluding Rice of course. The Great White North mostly produces wheat – 37,529,600 metric tons. The second most produced Canadian grain type is maize, which comes to 14,193,800 metric tons, then barley at 10,237,100 metric tons and finally soybeans with 5,358,900 metric tons.

"The numbers with their magic moving are creating so much diversity in life of people about every phenomenon of life. Those numbers with their game are keeping their big mystery inside itselves while are doing big impact in every process on our lovely Earth planet.

Those numbers with their games when are going in amount of up and down also are changing so many concepts to the brain of people for life and for environment, for their existence. So many phenomena influenced by the numbers' game have changed the map of the world.

After every war came big change on our planet so many countries separated by their Federate Union and won their Independence, so many others countries got out of their labeled name colony and became independent while created their Republic while separated one and for all from different Royal system.

How many countries have gained independence from the UK? Since than a total of 62 countries have gained independence from the United Kingdom (British Empire).

In 1939 Canada, South Africa, Australia New Zealand were the first to be given independence with Commonwealth.

This is followed by France with 28, Spain with 17, The Soviet Union with 16, Portugal with 7 and the USA with 5. All records listed on website are current and up-to-date.

The main reason that sent those countries to seek independence was higher taxation and frontier policy by British Empire.

So, when they rose up taxes and made so much strict their policy that was giving hard time to people of their colony this caused protest until to separate by them with strong fighting and to create their Republic Independent.

In this time again numbers were playing big impact with their mystery about changing social politic map of the world.

When million people won their freedom came another situation by numbers because those people can express more freely their thoughts and their innovation that will send them to develop economy with so many new modern branches while to build really modern city or town of their country.

Many new free independent countries created so much diversity and so many rivals about economy and science that send the world in another phase of development.

Innovation and creative ideas about science and art by people came in high level that changed the world in drastic way.

Really not only those phenomenon but and tragic phenomenon like Pandemic of "Covid 19" that gave death to 4,900.000 people in our Earth planet created new concept for life, that "Human's life 'is very important than anything else.

This new concept realized one union and solidarity between people between different countries and between continents on Earth planet.

As result different countries produced millions and millions of vaccines to save people's life while were helping and cooperating with each other.

These big numbers of death millions created new concept for people about protecting their health from all viruses, with prophylactic measures, like distance from each other, cleaning and using mask.

The numbers' game is impacting the people's life. Really originated of number is coming from two countries like India and Arabia that needed to use for astronomer in older past time.

It was around the 6 century, around this time that the great India astronomer Aryabhatta, invented as set of numerlc that those numbers are used by all around the world. (by Bhaswati Ghosh).

People, might already have heard that zero was invented in India. But it is not so widely known that even the other numerals were invented in India only. This is because the figures written as 1, 2, 3 etc. are commonly known as 'Arabic'.

This would naturally make it seem that the number system originated in Arabia and not in India. Sounds rather mysterious, no?

That something that was invented by an Indian scientist should be known as Arabic? But there's quite an interesting story behind this.

Sometime in the year 771, Arab merchants took some Indian scholars to Baghdad (the present capital of Iraq) to help teach them the new set of numbers. After learning the numbers, the Arabs translated the numbers into their own script that is Arabic.

Sometime later, the Arab traders carried a book of these numerals (in their language or script) to Europe, where the numbers were translated into Latin. As the world at large got these numbers from Arabia, these came to be known as Arabic.

In fact, it is interesting to note that there is another number system in use. This is the 'Roman' numerical system. The numbers in this system are written as I, II, III, IV, V etc. Although this number system is also a well-developed one, there's one problem in it. Since there is no symbol for zero in it, there is difficulty in carrying out addition, subtraction and other calculations.

Let's take an example. In the Arabic number system, the calculation of 2076+600, can be easily computed by arranging the numbers in two vertical columns;

However, the same calculation is not so easy, when it comes to the Roman system. Why? Because under the Roman system the numbers are written differently. This is because M means a thousand, D stands for 500, C stands for a hundred, L for fifty, X for ten, V for five and I for one.

It is amazing what a big difference the seemingly simple and valueless number '0' can make. The small number '1' can be turned into a million! a billion!! or even a trillion!!! – Thanks to the magical powers of zero.

Here are some more interesting facts. The script of the Arabic language (not mathematical) moves from right to left, unlike English, which moves from left to right. However, Arabic numbers are written from left to right. Why? Because they were borrowed from India!

Since the time they were invented, Arabic numerals have undergone only minor changes from the original Hindu manuscript. The numbers that have undergone slight changes include 4, 5, 6 and 7.

Whatever to be numbers Arabic, Indian or Roman their power on human life's is giving so much impact, because every change of those numbers in positive way or negative way is changing life of people for good or bad too.

If the population in one town or city is growing up rapidly, will come behind itself so many other problems in human life. Because of increased population, will face water shortage.

Increased industrial the community will waste air, water and land pollution. If science's people are multiplying this problem a dozen fold and they can see how it is going to have a global effect. Also, difficulties in the implementation of state development programs, increased instances of crime too.

Here, population growth refers to the increase in the number of individuals across the world. According to research, the last two centuries witnessed population explosion with the number increasing from 1 billion in the year 1800 to 7.6 billion in 2017 and various studies expect this number to surpass 10 billion post-2050.

Prior to the 19th century, people lacked medical facilities and death rates were high. With the advancement of the science and medicines, the death rates declined and high birth rates in the 19th and 20th century led to the population growth.

And the same reasons are still keeping the numbers high. While the developed countries have seen low numbers in last few decades, developing and poor countries growth rates are rising.

The impact of population growth varies with world region. It has become increasingly important over the past few decades that we increase production of vegetables, fruits and anything else us humans need to consume in order to live, lest we end up in a shortage that could drive up the price.

Positive effects of population growth:

Population growth contributes to the new inventions and growth of a country.

Enhances nation security.

Population growth contributes to the new inventions and growth of a country. Enhances nation security Today, civilians in several small nations such as South Korea have to carry mandatory military service.

To maintain the integrity of a nation during war, the government necessitates these services among public. Such practices do not take place in countries with high population growth.

With more civilians at hands, the government gets the opportunity to choose the physically fit soldiers to keep the country secured from external disturbances. In this way, population growth helps in boosting nation's solidarity.

Technological innovations. High population means the huge number of brains. More demand of every basic necessity in such countries encourages these brains to bring new ideas to fulfill required needs of a nation. Green Revolution in India in the 1970s is a fair example of innovative technology.

The increasing food demand led to the invention of High Yield variety seeds which doubled the production and maintained food security of the country. Also, today's popular IT technologies developed in countries with high population growth.

Economic benefits. Population growth provides numerous business opportunities. It leads to increase in demand for goods and services. And this demand encourages businessmen to try their luck in manufacturing the products and compete in the market.

The countries with high production in specific goods gain monetary benefits by exporting them. Increase in the labor force makes a country capable and enhances its infrastructure advancement.

Negative effects of population growth:

Numerous factors stimulate government to enact laws in limiting population growth.

Unemployment

Unemployment is an important cause of the overpopulation. With an increase in the number of individuals for few jobs, the competition rises, and a small amount gets an employment. And those jobs are either disguised or an underemployment.

Many developing and under-developed countries face this problem as they do not possess required infrastructure and facilities to generate employment for masses. Also, the rates of living standard, diseases, and suicides are high, in these countries.

Food security issues

A nutritious food and a 3 meals-a-day is a major problem arises with the population growth. As food is a basic requirement of an individual, the demand increases with population.

The government of countries with low capacity and cropping area finds difficulty in fulfilling these demands. At times, these countries have to import grains in a large amount, which results in limiting the budget set for the profitable development. And the high pressure on the available food stock engenders inadequate supply, which leads to malnourishment and diseases, thereafter.

Environment degradation.

History shows that high food demand changed the forests into the cultivable lands. Low forest area means decreased wildlife, which increases animals-humans conflict at the boundary regions. Also, cutting of forest leads to unanticipated climate changes, which impact the human life and settlements. The population growth enhances the limited natural resources use such as coal and petroleum, which degrades the environment in the form of air, soil, and water pollution.

Low per capita income

For a balanced per capita income, the economic and population growth must go hand in hand. In countries, where population growth rate exceeds economic growth, the per capita income lowers. This, in turn, minimizes the savings and lowers the living standard among the general population.

Lower land-man ratio.

The agriculture sector employs maximum labor force in developing countries. In countries such as India, the overpopulation in rural areas has led to the land fragmentation. This leads to the lowering land-man ratio, which means low income per head, a foremost cause of poverty.

Poverty.

With population growth, the demand for every basic good increase. This demand leads to inflation, which means higher spending on necessities. The low income and high price increase cost of living, which drags an individual to poverty.

Many studies criticize population growth, as it impacts a nation's self-reliance to great extent. Today, the population across the world is increasing at alarming rate. The concern regarding its consequences is fair but the need of an hour is to find the solutions to limit them.

At first, the developing/ underdeveloped countries with high growth rate such as India, Nigeria must bring out the government policies and create awareness among masses regarding the issues arising from overpopulation.

Also, the negative effects can only be minimized if government and citizens work together to achieve the same goal.

Mount of numbers are showing in civilization world the importance of town or city, also in industrial world is showing the importance of big factory, or plant or big industry what kind to be, while in agriculture is showing about how powerful one country in livestock is, dairy products, or in producing grain corns, or industrial plants like sugar beets or tabaco also is showing up how powerful, is any country about systematization of the ground and rural environment too.

While with huge numbers of producing like cars or new technology specific electronic technology or electronic supplies is giving bold label to them around this planet.

While about education Institution like Colleges or Universities, while the numbers of students is growing up every years and this huge numbers is increase, not decrease with years definitely the College or University is taking good name and big importance while is giving big impact and to city or town about their honor name and big reputation so is coming for that big good label.

From all those phenomena, we understand that our world and life is depended by those numbers, while with their moving up and down is reflecting direct in our daily life, about prosperity, happiness or opposite of those like poverty or desperation.

With their deep mystery number are main factor in developing of economy of every country. With numbers' s game is changing in different time, the situation in different countries of this planet, while during this numbers game is creating one conglomerate with full diversities of different phenomenon in our lovely Earth planet.

So many people are skeptical about this "Numbers' Game "while, they are thinking that phenomenon are happening because so is life, but really phenomenon are happening when the balance of this numbers' game is changing.

Every number has its mystery does not matter from the value or amount that has in itself, because is big mystery, how number zero that is empty number but so many zeros creating one supersize numbers that is bringing if and after number one (1) but there are bringing $ million, $ trillion and $ milliard.

MILITARY.

As we know the military is important asset of every nation. The military protect its citizen through its domestic and foreign policies while is enforcing them.

Through the military the Government is ensuring National security that is government duty, while is protecting and ensuring the security of citizens, the economy of its county and all institutions.

National security is very important and requires so huge budget, through this budget is to build and maintains the military spending. The total military expenditure in 2020 was about $1, 981Trillion.

Expenses of military also military size depended by the country size and military in needs. China, India and U.S.A. have the largest military size on Earth planet.

A majority countries on our planet have military only 36 countries do not have military. Most of the countries have mandatory military services. More interesting is that are some countries with number of people more small than their number of expenses of military this is not good math, because their country is small in square meter, and its population is small so why is so big their expenses of Military, this calculation is not efficient.

The first country on earth planet is the U.S.A. that has the highest military spending that any other nation. Its military expenses are for Department of Defense, regular activities, war spending, nuclear weapons, international military assistance and other Pentagon – related spending.

In 2020 the U.S.A was on top of list of countries expenses for military with total amount $ 778 billion more than any other country on this Earth planet.

The ten countries with the highest military expenditures are:

1- **The United States ($778 billion)**

2- **China ($252 billion [estimated])**

3- **India ($72.9 billion)**

4- **-Russia ($61.7 billion)**

5- **United Kingdom ($59.2 billion)**

6- **Saudi Arabia ($57.5 billion [estimated])**

7- **Germany ($52.8 billion)**

8- **France ($52.7 billion)**

9- **Japan ($49.1 billion)**

10- **South Korea ($45.7 billion)**

As mentioned previously, the United States spends more on its military than any other nation. The country's $778 billion military expenditure is among the expensive government programs, along with Social Security and Medicare.

The U.S. has the third-largest military with 1.367 million members on active duty and another 1.037 million in the National Guard and reserves. Following the United States is China, spending $252 billion and India, spending $72.9 billion.

Country
Spending (USD $)
2021 Population

Spending 2021

	U.S.D. $	Population.
United States	$750.00 Bn	332,915,073
China	$237.00 Bn	1,444,216,107
Saudi Arabia	$67.60 Bn	35,340,683
India	$61.00 Bn	1,393,409,038
United Kingdom	$55.10 Bn	68,207,116
Germany	$50.00 Bn	83,900,473
Japan	$49.00 Bn	126,050,804
Russia	$48.00 Bn	145,912,025
South Korea	$44.00 Bn	51,305,186
France	$41.50 Bn	65,426,179
Italy	$27.80 Bn	60,367,477
Brazil	$27.80 Bn	213,993,437
Australia	$26.30 Bn	25,788,215
United Arab Emirates	$22.75 Bn	9,991,089
Canada	$22.50 Bn	38,067,903
Israel	$20.00 Bn	8,789,774
Iran	$19.60 Bn	85,028,759

Turkey	$19.00 Bn	85,042,738
Spain	$15.10 Bn	46,745,216
Algeria	$13.00 Bn	44,616,624
Netherlands	$12.42 Bn	17,173,099
Poland	$12.00 Bn	37,797,005
Afghanistan	$12.00 Bn	39,835,428
Pakistan	$11.40 Bn	225,199,937
Singapore	$11.20 Bn	5,896,686
Egypt	$11.20 Bn	104,258,327
Taiwan	$10.72 Bn	23,855,010
Colombia	$10.60 Bn	51,265,844
Morocco	$10.00 Bn	37,344,795
Oman	$8.69 Bn	5,223,375
Indonesia	$7.60 Bn	276,361,783
Norway	$7.18 Bn	5,465,630
Thailand	$7.10 Bn	69,950,850
Angola	$7.00 Bn	33,933,610
Mexico	$7.00 Bn	130,262,216
Kuwait	$6.83 Bn	4,328,550
Sweden	$6.33 Bn	10,160,169
Qatar	$6.00 Bn	2,930,528
Vietnam	$5.50 Bn	98,168,833
Ukraine	$5.40 Bn	43,466,819
Romania	$5.05 Bn	19,127,774
Switzerland	$5.00 Bn	8,715,494
Uruguay	$4.95 Bn	3,485,151
Belgium	$4.92 Bn	11,632,326
Greece	$4.84 Bn	10,370,744
Denmark	$4.76 Bn	5,813,298
New Zealand	$4.30 Bn	4,860,643
South Africa	$4.28 Bn	60,041,994
Chile	$4.25 Bn	19,212,361

Argentina	$4.20 Bn	45,605,826
Kazakhstan	$4.00 Bn	18,994,962
Malaysia	$4.00 Bn	32,776,194
Bangladesh	$3.80 Bn	166,303,498
Finland	$3.57 Bn	5,548,360
Philippines	$3.47 Bn	111,046,913
Austria	$3.38 Bn	9,043,070
Portugal	$3.36 Bn	10,167,925
Libya	$3.00 Bn	6,958,532
Czech Republic	$2.97 Bn	10,724,555
Azerbaijan	$2.81 Bn	10,223,342
Myanmar	$2.65 Bn	54,806,012
Jordan	$2.60 Bn	10,269,021
Peru	$2.56 Bn	33,359,418
Lebanon	$2.50 Bn	6,769,146
Ecuador	$2.50 Bn	17,888,475
Sri Lanka	$2.50 Bn	21,497,310
Sudan	$2.47 Bn	44,909,353
Nigeria	$2.15 Bn	211,400,708
Slovakia	$2.12 Bn	5,460,721
Hungary	$2.08 Bn	9,634,164
Syria	$1.80 Bn	18,275,702
Iraq	$1.73 Bn	41,179,350
Tajikistan	$1.60 Bn	9,749,627
North Korea	$1.60 Bn	25,887,041
Bahrain	$1.42 Bn	1,748,296
Yemen	$1.40 Bn	30,490,640
Armenia	$1.39 Bn	2,968,127
Lithuania	$1.11 Bn	2,689,862
Bulgaria	$1.08 Bn	6,896,663
Uzbekistan	$975.00 Mn	33,935,763
Uganda	$935.00 Mn	47,123,531

Serbia	$907.00 Mn	8,697,550
Ireland	$870.00 Mn	4,982,907
Croatia	$800.00 Mn	4,081,651
Dominican Republic	$760.00 Mn	10,953,703
Venezuela	$745.00 Mn	28,704,954
Latvia	$724.00 Mn	1,866,942
Republic of the Congo	$715.00 Mn	5,657,013
Ghana	$710.00 Mn	31,732,129
Estonia	$685.00 Mn	1,325,185
Bolivia	$660.00 Mn	11,832,940
Cambodia	$604.00 Mn	16,946,438
Slovenia	$581.00 Mn	2,078,724
Tunisia	$550.00 Mn	11,935,766
Ivory Coast	$550.00 Mn	27,053,629
Namibia	$505.00 Mn	2,587,344
Panama	$500.00 Mn	4,381,579
Cuba	$500.00 Mn	11,317,505
Botswana	$450.00 Mn	2,397,241
Ethiopia	$350.00 Mn	117,876,227
Cameroon	$347.00 Mn	27,224,265
Georgia	$327.00 Mn	3,979,765
Albania	$250.00 Mn	2,872,933
Paraguay	$250.00 Mn	7,219,638
Mozambique Mn	$245.00	32,163,047
Guatemala	$240.00 Mn	18,249,860
Tanzania	$223.00 Mn	61,498,437
Nepal	$213.00 Mn	29,674,920
Honduras	$205.00 Mn	10,062,991
Turkmenistan	$200.00 Mn	6,117,924
Chad	$200.00 Mn	16,914,985
El Salvador	$167.00 Mn	6,518,499
Bosnia And Herzegovin	$165.00 Mn	3,263,466

Mongolia	$155.00 Mn	3,329,289
Nicaragua	$140.00 Mn	6,702,385
Burkina Faso	$130.00 Mn	21,497,096
Kenya	$121.00 Mn	54,985,698
Madagascar	$115.00 Mn	28,427,328
North Macedonia	$108.15 Mn	2,082,658
Zimbabwe	$100.00 Mn	15,092,171
DR Congo	$100.00 Mn	92,377,993
Gabon	$83.00 Mn	2,278,825
South Sudan	$80.00 Mn	11,381,378
Sierra Leone	$75.50 Mn	8,141,343
Mali	$70.00 Mn	20,855,735
Montenegro	$65.00 Mn	628,053
Suriname	$63.00 Mn	591,800
Somalia	$62.20 Mn	16,359,504
Mauritania	$50.25 Mn	4,775,119
Zambia	$40.00 Mn	18,920,651
Moldova	$30.00 Mn	4,024,019
Bhutan	$25.12 Mn	779,898
Central African Republic	$20.00 Mn	4,919,981
Kyrgyzstan	$20.00 Mn	6,628,356
Laos	$18.50 Mn	7,379,358
Liberia	$13.00 Mn	5,180,203
Belarus	$623.70	9,442,862

This numbers' game is showing with its capriccio and with full irony how so many countries are playing in international field about spending money for military while their population is so many times smaller than their expenses or military's people or equipment's.

This big amount of money that are spent for military all around the world and are produced so many equipment's and supplies of military I do not know how that earth planet is not burn or is not got poison?

...but Universe has big power to clean our air with its magic phenomenon, because the rain can make recycle and aspire of poison to the air, but thanks to superpower of the great universe with its super chemical phenomenon is cleaning for really our atmosphere.

So many countries with big expenses is going around $ 1700 trillion while others around $21 billion, in electronic monitor is blocked from this big numbers where to find numbers for those expense, and Universe is smiling and Cometa Halley that is flying with speed cosmic is getting shocking for the speed and lock for moment by this supe huge numbers in this electronic monitor.

The numbers' game is showing its power with irony after all this big show where so money people are hungry so many people are suffering for medicine and so many are going until to the end of their life full of debts by their home or by their other debts of education of medical services, also so many never has their own home in their life or no home at all.

If one building is costing $ one million to $ five million how many new towns or cities will be built with those around $1860 Trillion by country that have large expenditure of military, or more less with those countries that their expenses for military calculated with $ million but totally is being to $ 21 billion.

This is simple equation for people with brilliant mind in our Earth planet. At least 170 super modern cities will be built on earth planet while to calculate to some countries has not so much expensive product and labor forces.

The world's 10 longest railway networks

The United States has the world's longest railway network, followed by China and India. Railway-technology.com profiles the 10 largest railway networks in the world based on total operating A plan is in place to build a 27,000km national high speed rail system in four phases by 2030.

Construction of the California high-speed rail, the country's first high-speed rail project, was well underway by the beginning of 2014.

Three more high-speed projects including the Midwest high-speed rail line connecting Chicago with Indianapolis or St. Louis, Texas high-speed rail, and the Northeast High-Speed Corridor are under development.

The US rail network, with an operating route length over 250,000km, is the biggest in the world. Freight lines constitute about 80% of the country's total rail network, while the total passenger network spans about 35,000km.

The US freight rail network consists of 538 railroads (seven Class I railroads, 21 regional railroads, and 510 local railroads) operated by private organizations.

Union Pacific Railroad and BNSF (British Naval Standard Forces) Railway are among the largest freight railroad networks in the world.

BNSF Railway (reporting mark BNSF) (British Naval Standard Forces) is the largest freight railroad network in North America.

One of nine North American Class I railroads, BNSF has 41,000 employees, 32,500 miles (52,300 km) of track in 28 states, and more than 8,000 locomotives.

The national passenger rail network Amtrak comprises of more than 30 train routes connecting 500 destinations across 46 American states.

China: 100,000km

China's rail network, with a route length of over 100,000km, ranks as the second biggest rail network in the world. The extensive network, operated by state-owned China Railway Corporation, carried 2.08 billion passengers (the second highest after Indian Railways) and 3.22 billion tons of freight (the second highest after the US railway network) in 2013.

Rail is the principal mode of transport in China. The country's rail network consists of over 90,000km of conventional rail routes and approximately 10,000km of high-speed lines.

The total rail network of the country is targeted to exceed 270,000km by 2050.

The rapid expansion of China's high-speed rail network in recent years makes it by far the largest in the world.

The 2,298km Beijing – Guangzhou high speed line is the world's longest high-speed railway line. The total length of China's high-speed rail network is projected to reach 50,000km by 2020.

Russia:

85,500km, Russia's whole network, operated by state-owned monopoly Russian Railways (RZD), runs for over 85,500km.

In 2013, the network carried 1.08 billion passengers and 1.2 billion tons of freight – the third highest freight volume after the US and China.

The Russian railway network incorporates12 main lines, many of which provide direct connections to the European and Asian national railway systems such as Finland, France, Germany, Poland, China, Mongolia and North Korea.

The Trans-Siberian Railway (the Moscow-Vladivostok line), spanning a length of 9,289km, is the longest and one of the busiest railway lines in the world.

RZD introduced the Sapsan high-speed rail service between St. Petersburg and Moscow in 2009, but it has not proved successful due to sharing existing lines with low-speed train operations.

A dedicated high-speed corridor between the two cities has been planned with a proposed investment of $35bn. RZD expects to have 2,500km of high-speed rail between Moscow and Kiev, Minsk and Kursk by 2015.

India:

65,000kmThe Indian nationwide rail network, the fourth longest in the world, is owned and operated by state-owned Indian Railways and includes an operating route length of more than 65,000km. The network carried about eight billion passengers (the highest in the world) and 1.01 million tons of freight (fourth highest in the world) in 2013.

The Indian railway network is divided into 17 zones and operates more than 19,000 trains per day, including 12,000 passenger trains and 7,000 freight trains.

The national railway operator plans to add 4,000km of new lines by 2017, as well as significant gauge conversion, doubling and electrification of its existing aging lines.

It also plans to add 3,338km of exclusive freight network by 2017 with the implementation of Eastern & Western Dedicated

Freight Corridors (DFC), two of the six identified dedicated freight corridors in India.

Six high-speed corridors have also been identified for implementation in the country. The 534km Mumbai-Ahmedabad high-speed link is being advanced as a pilot project with an estimated investment of $9.65bn.

Canada:

48,000kmCanada's 48,000km of rail lines makes its national network the fifth longest in the world. Canadian National Railway (CN) and Canadian Pacific Railway (CPR) are the two major freight rail networks operating in the country, while Via Rail operates the 12,500km intercity passenger rail service.

Algoma Central Railway and Ontario Northland Railway are among the other smaller railways providing passenger services to certain rural areas in the country.

Three Canadian cities – Montreal, Toronto and Vancouver – have extensive commuter train systems. In addition, the Rocky Mountaineer and Royal Canadian Pacific offer luxury rail tours to view the scenic beauty of certain mountainous areas in the country.

Canada, however, does not have a single high-speed line on its railway network. Many high-speed lines such as Toronto-Montreal, Calgary-Edmonton and Montreal-Boston have been proposed, but none of these have progressed beyond preliminary studies as of January 2014.

Germany:

41,000kmState-owned Deutshe Bahn dominates Germany's 41,000km railway network, accounting for about 80% of the total freight traffic and 99% of the long-distance passenger traffic.

More than 150 private railway companies apart from Deutshe Bahn operate on the network, providing regional passenger and freight services. The S-Bahn serves major suburban areas, while the Hamburg Cologne Express (HKX) is the major long-distance passenger operator after Deutshe Bahn.

The German railway network had more than 1,300km of high-speed railway track operational as of mid-2013 and more than 400km of new high-speed line under construction.

Deutshe Bahn opened high-speed services, under the name InterCity Express (ICE), for the first time in 1991. The high-speed network, operated at speeds up to 320km/h, now connects major German cities and neighboring countries such as France, Switzerland, Belgium, the Netherlands and Austria.

Australia:

40,000kmThe Australian railway network is the world's seventh longest at more than 40,000km. Most of the railway network infrastructure is owned and maintained by the Australian government either at the federal or state level. The majority of the trains on the network are, however, operated by private companies.

Aurizon (formerly QR National), Genesee and Wyoming Australia, and Pacific National are among the major freight operators on the network. Great Southern Railway, NSW TrainLink and Queensland Rail are the leading long-distance passenger rail operators. Metro Trains Melbourne, Sydney Trains, V/Line and Adelaide Metro operate commuter passenger services in major suburban areas. In addition, a number of private mining railways operate in the country.

The Australian railway network does not have a high-speed line yet. A high-speed rail network connecting Brisbane, Sydney,

Canberra and Melbourne is proposed to be built with an estimated capital cost of $114bn,

(billion) but the first phase of the 1,748km high-speed network will not be realized before 2035.

Argentina:

36,000km, Argentina's current rail network spanning over 36,000km in length ranks the eighth largest in the world. Argentina used to have about 47,000km of rail network at the end of the Second World War, mostly operated by British and French-owned railway companies.

But the decline of profits and the rise of highway construction in the subsequent decades reduced the network to the 36,000km of line that exists today. The railway companies operating on the network were nationalized in 1948 with the creation of the state railroad corporation Ferrocarriles - Argentinos.

The Argentinean railway was privatized between 1992 and 1995 with the grant of concessions to different private companies for operating six divisions of the formerly state-owned rail network.

Cities such as Buenos Aires, Resistencia and Mendoza offer extensive suburban passenger services, as well as the long-distance passenger lines in the country.

The much talked-about Argentine high-speed railway is not a reality yet. An announcement was made in 2006 to develop a 310km high-speed line between Buenos Aires and Rosario.

The project was, however, not implemented as of 2013. A second high-speed line stretching 400km between Rosario and Cordoba has also been proposed.

France:

29,000km At 29,000km, the French railway network is the second biggest in Europe and the ninth biggest in the world. The French railway network is predominantly passenger-centric and more than 50% of the country's lines are electrified. State-owned Société Nationale des Chemins de fer Français (SNCF) is the principal railway operator in the country.

The country's high-speed long distance passenger services are known as Train à Grande Vitesse (TGV) and the standard long-distance passenger services are branded Intercités. The short and middle distance passenger rail services are known as Transport Express Régional (TER). The network offers linkages to adjacent countries such as Belgium, Italy and the UK.

France was one of the early adopters of high-speed rail technology; SNCF brought into operation the TGV high-speed rail in 1981. The country's current high-speed network exceeds a length of 1,550km. The Tours-Bordeaux high-speed rail project, which is due for completion in 2017, will add another 302km into the network.

Brazil:

28,000kmThe first railway line in Brazil became operational in 1984. The railway network was nationalized in 1957 with the creation of Rede Ferroviária Federal Sociedade Anônima (RFFSA). The country's railway network was divided into different services to be operated by a range of private and public operators by 2007.

The 28,000km network is predominantly freight-focused and includes major iron ore rail lines. The country's passenger rail services are mostly concentrated in urban and suburban areas. Eight Brazilian cities have metro systems, São Paulo Metro being the biggest among them.

In 2012, the Brazilian government announced the construction of 10,000km of new lines comprised of freight and high-speed passenger lines by 2042. A 511km high-speed rail link between São Paulo and Rio de Janeiro has been planned for development in the country, but the project is yet to take off.

What scenario around the world it is showing this Number's Game while with its power is doing big impact in life of people. Universe with all his numbers of planets and all his super huge number of stars with its energy is giving one big impact with its numbers in different stages of life of people on Earth planet. So the number's game power is absolute and not to doubt about effecting of life of people.

Durime P. Zherka
Friday. Time : 4;02.p.m.
Fort Lauderdale.Fl., U.S.A.

Printed in the United States
by Baker & Taylor Publisher Services